AFRICAN LIFE

AND

CUSTOMS

Edward Wilmot Blyden, LL.D.

Black Classic Press

African Life and Customs

First published 1908
Reprinted from
The Sierra Leone Weekly News
Published by Black Classic Press, 1994
All rights reserved
L. C. Card Number: 93-74113
ISBN 0933121-43-1
Cover art and design by Carles Juzang

Printed on acid free paper to assure long life

Founded in 1978, Black Classic Press specializes in bringing to light obscure and significant works by and about people of African descent. If our books are not available in your area, ask your local bookseller to order them. Our current list of titles can be obtained by writing:

Black Classic Press
c/o List
P.O. Box 13414
Baltimore, MD 21203

PREFACE.

THE following pages have been written with the desire, if possible, of unfolding the African, who has received unmixed European culture, to himself, through a study of the customs of his fathers, and also of assisting the European political overlord, ruling in Africa, to arrive at a proper appreciation of conditions.

It is now recognised on all hands that the usefulness, true progress, and happiness of the African, and the success of the European in Africa, depend largely, if not entirely, upon the accurate knowledge on the part of the latter of the people and country which he is attempting to exploit.

It has been thought best to retain the form of the chapters as they appeared in the *Sierra Leone Weekly News.*

E. W. B.

DEDICATION.

THE AUTHOR

CONSIDERS IT A PRIVILEGE TO DEDICATE THIS

LITTLE BOOK

AS A SINCERE EXPRESSION OF THE
HIGHEST ADMIRATION FOR CHARACTER AND ABILITY,

TO

WILLIAM JOHN DAVEY, ESQUIRE,

FOR THIRTY YEARS A PARTNER IN THE FIRM OF

MESSRS. ELDER, DEMPSTER & Co.,

AND WHOSE UNREMITTING AND EFFECTIVE LABOURS
IN THE CAUSE OF AFRICA'S ENLIGHTENMENT AND
PROGRESS, DURING A PERIOD OF NEARLY FORTY
YEARS, ENTITLE HIM TO THE GRATITUDE AND ESTEEM

OF

ALL AFRICANS.

Though we are in a great measure responsible for the happiness and destiny of millions of our backward fellow countrymen in South Africa, we have done little, as a body of white rulers, to study native thought, aspiration and custom. Instead of investigating facts, we have been occupied with opinions, and have looked at the natives through the eyes of home sentiment or dividends.—DUDLEY KIDD *in* "*Kafir Socialism.*"

———

It is a pity that our Government, in its dealing with native races, has no Bureau of Ethnology or Advisory Board of Anthropologists to consult. If it had it might have been saved from many blunders which have cost the nation dear in blood and treasure.—Dr. J. G. FRAZER *in* " *Daily Mail.*"

———

In Africa it really would be money in our pockets to understand the native law and custom, which is elaborate and complex, and can scarcely be disregarded with impunity. —ANDREW LANG *in* " *Morning Post.*",

AFRICAN LIFE AND CUSTOMS.

CHAPTER I.

UNTIL the close of the Civil War in America the Slave Power had shaped the conceptions of the Western World as to the African, his character, possibilities, and destiny. Divines and politicians, physiologists and scientists, exhausted the resources of their intellect in the endeavour to prove the Negro only *quasi*-human—an excellent animal, but only an animal—born to serve a superior race.

But the close of the nineteenth century and the beginning of the twentieth have brought to the front a new school of thinkers on African and racial questions. Among these Mary Kingsley leads the way, owing to her original studies in the home of the African. She has been followed by such students as Lady Lugard, J. E. Dennett, Major Leonard, Dudley Kidd, Sir Sydney Olivier, Governor of Jamaica, M. Finot, Editor of *La Revue* in Paris, and Rome Hall.

Mary Kingsley among other writings gave us " West African Studies." Lady Lugard has given us "A Tropical Dependency," Mr. Dennett, "Back of the Black Man's Mind." Major Leonard, " The Lower Niger and its Tribes." Mr. Dudley Kidd, " The Essential Kafir" and " Savage Childhood."*

* Mr. Kidd has recently followed these works by his most illuminating book on " Kafir Socialism."

Sir Sydney Olivier has given us "White Capital and Coloured Labour." M. Finot, "Race Prejudice," and Dr. Rome Hall his experiences in West Africa in the *West African Mail.*

These writers, most of whom have been conscientious investigators on the spot, have broken through the sinister traditions of hundreds of years, and are teaching their countrymen to judge the Man of Africa by the impartial light of truth, and not from the standpoint of prejudice and preconceived ideas. They have rejected the theories of the noisy and blustering anthropologists of forty or fifty years ago—the Notts and Gliddons, Burtons, Winwood Reade, Hunt, *et id omme genus* —who invented all sorts of arguments based upon estimates of physical phenomena as conceived by phrenology or physiognomy, using signs and symbols taken from every part of the man—from the heel to the skull—to prove the mental and moral inferiority of the Negro. No attempt was made to prove his *physical* inferiority, because it was manifest that, although he has not developed as rapidly in the sciences and the arts as some other sections of the human race, yet he is physically the most vigorous portion of the human family—"put up" to stand all climates and conditions.

With regard to arguments drawn from physical appearance to prove human inferiority, M. Finot has established their utter absurdity, and has shown that in all the essentials of real manhood, physical, intellectual and moral—the Negro is not inferior to any other section of the human race, and is capable of equal development and progress under conditions similar to those which have contributed to the development of the more advanced portions of mankind—that is to say, he is in no way less capable of playing well the part assigned to him in the great *drama* of the world's life than any other section of humanity, granting him equal conditions of mental and moral growth. M. Finot, in his great work, p. 35, says :—

The conclusion forces itself upon us that there are no inferior and superior races, but only races living outside or within the influences of culture. The appearance of civilisation and its evolution among certain white peoples, and within a certain geographical latitude is only the effect of circumstances.

It is not contended that the work of the Negro will be identical with that of other races ; there is no moral or material necessity for this. The African will never move in the direction, for example, in which Messrs. Edison and Marconi, Lord Lister, etc., are leaders. For him and his effective work in his own country, the intricacies of science and its marvellous achievements are neither accessible nor necessary. Owing to climatic conditions, discoveries in that direction are entirely impossible. Nor will he excel on the great political lines for successful pursuit in which the European has been naturally endowed. Politics as understood in Europe are not his *forte*. The African, at least in the present Age, is to pursue the calling of man when in his perfect state. But some may say the African is not in his perfect state. We admit this to some extent, but only where he has been interfered with by alien influence. His real work as we see it among the great tribes of the interior is to speak to the earth and let it teach him (Job. 12, 8)—to dress the garden and to keep it. In his normal state he does not envy those who live by exploiting the man of the soil. The first exploiter of the simple agriculturist, working innocently and un-suspectingly in the Garden of Eden, was that eminent and most ingenious of beings who is said to have led in the disloyal enterprise of the rebel Angels.

Chapter II.

THERE is no question now as to the human unity, but each section has developed for itself such a system or code of life as its environments have suggested—to be improved, not changed by larger knowledge. The African has developed and organised a system useful to him for all the needs of life.

It is our purpose to endeavour to describe in these articles the way he has constructed for himself his portion of the world. We shall deal with the social, industrial, and economic arrangements under which, evolved in the course of centuries, he has lived and thriven, generation after generation. And we must premise that we are dealing with the African pure and simple—the so-called Pagan African—the man untouched either by European or Asiatic influence.

The facts in this African life which we shall endeavour to point out are the following :—

1st. The Family, which in Africa, as everywhere else, is the basic unit of society. Every male and female marries at the proper age. Every woman is required and expects to perform her part of the function of motherhood—to do her share in continuing the human race.

2nd. Property. The land and the water are accessible to all. Nobody is in want of either, for work, for food, or for clothing.

3rd. Social Life. This is communistic or co-operative. All work for each, and each works for all.

4th. The tribes have laws regulating every function of human life and the laws are known to all the members of the tribe, and justice is administered by the tribal chiefs in the presence of the whole people in the village or town, where any violation of tribal law may have taken place. There is no need for Standing Armies. The whole people of the village or town are jointly and severally guardians and preservers of the peace.

The foundation of the African Family is plural marriage and, contrary to the general opinion, this marriage rests upon the will of the woman, and this will operates to protect from abuse the functional work of the sex, and to provide that all women shall share *normally* in this work with a view to healthy posterity and an unfailing supply of population.

It is less a matter of sentiment, of feeling, of emotion, than of duty, of patriotism. Compulsory spinsterhood is unknown under the African system. *That* is a creation of the West. Its existence here is abnormal, anticlimatic, and considered a monstrosity, as Miss Kingsley wittingly points out ; and is destined, wherever it seems to exist in practice, to disappear as an unscientific interference of good meaning foreign philanthropists with the natural conditions of the country.

The idea of increase of population in Africa, as in all Eastern countries, is first and foremost, as should be the case, and over-rides all other considerations. " Multiply and replenish " is older than any other

law—written not only in the books of men, but in
the " manuscripts of God," and will abide for ever,
outliving all other arrangements, which for local
convenience, have been adopted by man in other
regions of the earth.

In the temperate regions the climatic conditions
produce a periodical invigoration of exhausted
nature. For six months in the year Nature
furnishes a close season when vegetable and
animal life undergoes rest and recuperation. But
in Africa, while in the vegetable kingdom there are
brief periods, when the rains cease, during which
the leaves fall, the ground refuses to bring forth,
and Nature compels rest, in the animal kingdom,
where man has introduced his inventions there is
no rest, and it is difficult there without artificial
intervention for a first-class breed of animals to be
produced. Generations of experience have taught
this to the African ; and while he pays no attention
to the development of a good race of the brute
creation,—to the development of horses and cattle,
etc., as in Europe—he has learned the art of
producing, preserving and perpetuating under his
climatic conditions, the higher animal Man. He
has learnt for his country and race an effective
Stirpiculture or Eugenic system—which, if we are
to believe Dr. Francis Galton and Dr. Rentoul,
Europe is now striving to attain. For thousands of
years before Ethiopia had been meddled with by any
exotic interference her people were described as
long-lived, tall and handsome ; and this physical
perfection was the basis of moral excellence.
They were also described as "blameless Ethio-
pians" ; and so throughout the Soudan where the
higher tribes flourish, this system of stirpiculture
prevails. Ignorant people describe this system as
blighting, but by plural marriage they mean the

promiscuous sexual relations which are a burden, an opprobrium, and a problem to Europe.

It is not generally known that in connection with this system there is *among Africans* a regular process of education for male and female, for a period of at least three years, to prepare them for the life they are to follow, and the system under which they are to live.

In the Society for girls which goes by various names in different parts of Africa—called Bundo in our neighbourhood, and Suna further North among the Jolloffs—the teachers are women only : usually, the older women in the neighbourhood are selected for this office, but always women of experience. Instruction is given in everything which prepares a woman to act well her part in the existing social Order—everything necessary to enable the young mother to perform the function which her position involves. The women who impart these lessons are either married or aged widows, and unpaid. It is a labour which is a part of the communal work. Compare this with the system of employing paid *Spinsters* to train girls to be wives and mothers ! And to show that this latter system is not entirely satisfactory even in Europe where it was created, we quote the following from the London *Daily Mail*, September 2, 1905, under the heading, " Schools for Brides " :—

" Already there are places where future brides can be taught the management of a household, and if there were more of them the advantage would be great. A statistician who could compute how much money is wasted through ignorance by newly married couples would be able to produce some startling figures."

The *Christian World*, June 6, 1907, says :—

A school for mothers where they may receive practical training in the washing and feeding of babies, and the right treatment of their minor ailments has been opened at St. Pancras.

Dr. Saleeby, discussing the question of infant mortality a few months ago, said :—

The remedy was the establishment of schools for mothers, and seeing to the feeding of nursing mothers rather than the babes, which should be fed from the breast. By assisting and educating mothers in the care of their infants at the right time they would be adopting a method which would be found incomparably cheaper than supporting institutions to look after the sick and the weakly.

Africa has had these institutions from time immemorial. In the Bundo Society or School, as we have said above, instruction is given in all the normal and abnormal complaints and diseases to which women are liable, especially as wives and mothers ; and all the known remedies for the prevention and cure or alleviation of such diseases, are taught ; so that when a girl has passed through the prescribed course of training, she is prepared without extraneous aid, everywhere and at all times, in the bush or in the town, to take care of herself in emergencies. The irregularity of males attending to females under delicate circumstances very rarely occurs.

The Bundo Society is a most ancient Order of Women, whose origin no one knows, and no one in any of the tribes can imagine a time when the Society did not exist. All its offices, as we have said, are filled, all its rites and ceremonies are performed, and all its teachings are imparted by women only. There are no male pupils or male teachers.

The Porroh Society is a similar Order of Men. Some Europeans, missionaries and laymen, in the Sierra Leone Protectorate and elsewhere, have been admitted to membership in the Porroh Society. The time may come when European females may seek admission to the Bundo Society, then they will begin to understand how, from generation to generation, African mothers have produced the strong men who by their labours in the Western Hemisphere, as Sir Alfred Jones has recently reminded us, and on their own continent, have helped to create the wealth of Europe, and who to-day do all the hard, laborious outdoor work in our settlements. East, West and South in Africa—on land and on sea—the African system of stiripiculture has furnished nearly all the physical force which has enabled Europe to assert her ascendancy on this continent — soldiers who have saturated the earth on the coast and in the interior with their blood, carrying the Union Jack and the Tricolour to victory, and have laid the foundation of the military prestige which sustains British and French authority throughout the entire Soudan.

CHAPTER III.

BEFORE beginning the discussion to-day, we shall quote from Miss Mary Kingsley a passage which occurs in her last letter written for the public. It was addressed to an African paper, *The New Africa*, published at Monrovia, and written on her way to South Africa, whence, alas! she never returned. It is a voice from the grave. She says :—

"I know there is a general opinion among the leading men of both races that Christianity will give the one possible solution of the whole problem. I fail to be able to believe this. I fail to believe Christianity will bring peace between the two races, for the simple reason that, though it may be possible to convert Africans *en masse* into practical Christians, it is quite impossible to convert Europeans *en masse* to it. . . . So I venture to say that you who build on Christianity in this matter are not building on safe ground.   You cannot by talking about Christianity to the Europeans save your people.   I believe there is a thing you could appeal to more safely in the case of the Anglo-Saxon, particularly the English ; that thing is honour, the honour of a gentleman."

"I have had to stand up alone these two years and fight for Africa's freedom and institutions, while Africans equally well and better educated in English culture have been talking about religious matters, etc., to a pack of people who do not care for Christianity at all."

With reference to this the present writer in an address before the African Society in 1903 said :—

" If the African educated on European lines is unable or unwilling to teach the outside world something of the Institutions and inner feelings of his people ; if, for some reason or other, he can show nothing of his real self to those anxious to learn, and to assist him ; if he cannot make his friends feel the force of his racial character and sympathise with his racial aspiration, then it is evident that his education has been sadly defective, that his training by aliens has done but little for him—that his teachers have surely missed their aim and wasted their time."

To resume the subject.   Every African woman, as we have said, is required and expects to perform her part of the function of motherhood—to do her share of the work of continuing the human race, but like her European sister of the present day, she objects to being simply a child-bearing machine, and she demands a period of rest in conformity to the law of reserve which is still part of the law of increase among animals.   Mrs. Flora Steel—an English lady of ability and experience—discusses this question in her able article in the *Monthly Review* for April, 1906, on " *Marriage in the East and in the West.*"   This law of female reserve and recuperation which prevails everywhere in Eastern countries, the African woman has been taught by Nature and her training to follow, and she insists upon a period of three years continuous rest before taking up again the duties of motherhood. This rest in her exhausting climate preserves her physical strength and vigour, and secures like conditions in her offspring. To the Europeanized African woman these things seldom appeal, beguiled by the unnatural monopoly given to her by the Marriage Ceremony of the Church, she has come to believe that she needs no rest, that the cruel imposition upon her energies is a part of the order of Nature and so clings to a state of things which she knows is fraught with evil for herself and her children—so strong is the love of power and the charm of monopoly in the human heart.

When African girls have reached maturity and gone through the course of instruction to which we referred in our last, they are subjected before they leave the secret grove to the rite analogous to circumcision, which, in tropical countries, has an important bearing upon the welfare of mothers and their offspring. This rite is sometimes described in European medical works.

Here, then, we have a practical species of stripiculture or eugenics, whose operation extends back over centuries producing continuously a vigorous and prolific race of men and women ; and without which, in spite of what may be said or done, experience teaches that decay and death stare the African in the face. (*See Appendix B.*)

The system of the Pagan African family differs from the Islamic system where marriages are limited to four wives, who are considered legally entitled to all conjugal rights. The Pagan system resembles more the Hebrew system, where there was no fixed limit, only the general caution "not to multiply wives."

An important social advantage also accrues from the marriage system under consideration. The girls, on leaving the school in which they associated on the most intimate terms for years, are seldom willing to separate from their companions; and, with the communistic privilege which they enjoy, they often solicit the husbands assigned them on leaving school to take their most intimate friend as a mate. It is the duty in Africa, as in Oriental countries generally, of the father of a girl on her reaching maturity to find a husband for her, and it is equally the duty of the girl to accept the husband so provided. This is so ancient a custom and so generally understood that there is seldom any friction or inconvenience; and whenever there is, the girl is always sure of a husband. She must be taken in and sheltered if the man is able to take care of her, a matter always carefully looked into before the marriage is arranged. In this way the breaking up and disintegration of Society never takes place as under the European system. Native parents who follow European customs often grievously suffer from the breaking up of the family life which frequently occurs on the marriage of their daughters. A man whose business calls him to a distant part of Africa takes in marriage a girl just from school, in Sierra Leone for example, separates her from the associations of childhood, carries her to another part of the coast among a people whose language and customs are strange to her. It is often the case that the disappointed young wife pines, grieves and wastes away under privations, intellectual, social and physical, which her husband, however devoted, seldom understands; and one day news comes to her startled and stricken parents that Mary Ann or Regina is dead.

The latest issue of the *Lagos Record* to hand (September 21st) emphasises this subject in the following striking paragraph :

> The frequent deaths of young girls just on attaining to puberty is occasioning much anxiety with every section of the community. Two such deaths have occurred within the past ten days, while it is notorious that the native civilised girl can offer but little resistance to the strain of illness, and collapses at the least augmentation of disease. We are taking to the ways of civilisation, but it is at the penalty of having our children to become weaklings.

Besides, even where the child lives, the parents are deprived of their co-operative help which they would enjoy if the girl and her husband were on the spot. The Christian Natives, as a rùle, are compelled to work in isolation, under the individualistic system of Europe which, for the mass of the people, involves a hand-to-mouth existence. This will account in part for the lack of agricultural and industrial enterprise and the absence consequently, of productive usefulness in the Europeanized native, everywhere witnessed on the Coast, so as to give rise to the bitter taunt of even so good a friend of the African as Miss Kingsley, viz. :— that " the Missionary-made man is the Curse of the Coast." The lay European is often heard to say, " I don't know about missionaries, but I detest converts," and the missionary himself is often not free from this contempt of the work of his own hands.

Of course this unnatural and unsatisfactory state of things, which profits no one, in which nobody rejoices, cannot last always. Already there are signs of its disappearance ; and, in spite of the

tears and embraces with which its votaries cling to
it, they are powerless to retain it.   The words
inscribed on it are visible to any careful observer
and growing clearer and clearer every day—*Delenda
est Carthago.*

> Truth *crushed* to earth will *rise again ;*
> The eternal years of God are hers ;
> But error *wounded* writhes with pain
> And dies amid its worshippers.

Chapter IV.

WE begin again to-day with a quotation from
Miss Kingsley, because we believe that her words
ought to be deeply impressed upon the minds of
Africans as well as Europeans who have dealings
with this country.   She says :—

The subject of the relationship between European and African
culture is one in which I am quite deeply interested.

    .   .   .   .   .   .

The stay-at-home statesmen think that Africans are all awful
savages or silly children—people who can only be dealt with on a
reformatory penitentiary line.   This view you know is not mine,
nor that of the very small party—the scientific ethnologists—who
deal with Africa ; but it is the view of the statesmen and the
general public and the mission public in African affairs.

    .   .   .   .   .   .

There are thousands of Englishmen who would not destroy native
independence and institutions if they but knew what those things
really were ; who would respect native law if they knew what it
was, and who would give over sneering at the African and respect
him if they knew him as he is really and truly, as I have known
him.

    .   .   .   .   .   .

I believe that no race can, as a race, advance except on its own
line of development, and that it is the duty of England to preserve
the African nationalism and not destroy it, but destroy it she will
unless you who know it come forward and demonstrate that African
Nationalism is a good thing, and that it is not a welter of barbarism,

cannibalism and cruelty. . . . The Christian general public up here will bring little influence to bear on preserving native institutions. The public, be it granted, is a powerful one, but it has been taught that all African native institutions are bad, and unless you preserve your institutions, above all your *land law*, you cannot, no race can, preserve your liberty.

Each country has its own problems which must be solved by itself in spite of missionary theories, which have everywhere not only failed to do what they promised but have complicated matters by creating new problems strange to the people-- insoluble problems—whose effect has been far from favourable among the dark races of the earth.

Africa solved the marriage question for herself thousands of years ago. It has needed no revision and no amendment, because founded upon the law of Nature and not upon the *dictum* of any ecclesiastical heirachy. Europe is still grappling with the problem, and finds that not only is her solution unsatisfactory, but out of it have grown other difficult questions. " There is not one social question," said Gambetta, " there are *social questions.*"

This question is one which is so serious in its consequences in all tropical countries, that it cannot be too earnestly enquired into by those who have the welfare of the race at heart. The marriage laws of Europe have proved disastrous in the Equatorial regions of the globe ; and sooner or later the question must command much greater attention from the Imperial races than it has hitherto received.

These laws introduced into the West Indies have not been salutary. The debilitating effect of the climate has again and again been pointed out by European travellers. Miss Pullen-Burry in her work on "Jamaica as it is," published in 1903, makes the following suggestive remarks :—

I had intended to write a diary ; instead I have made some progress down that path which is said to be paved with good intentions. They say of the natives of these latitudes that " they were born tired, grew up tired, and have been tired ever since." I cannot truthfully say that of myself, although the enervating climate tries the strongest when they feel tropical heat for the first time. Energies which are rampant in the temperate zone find the end of their tether very soon under Jamaican skies. Perhaps this is why the island is said to be beneficial to persons suffering from overdone nerves. They must rest in the middle of the day ; the heat is too great for any exertion, p. 3.

A more recent observer, Mr. John Henderson, in his " Jamaica " published, 1906, says :—

At midday the West Indies present a picture of death. There is no movement, no life current. It is as though the island of Jamaica was scorched dead. The birds float like ragged strips of paper on the edge of the breeze which dies on its journey inland. Here, by the sea, the senses are lulled to sweet indifference to all things save the noise and coolness of the breeze. Jamaicans call this breeze the doctor ; it is the doctor that makes Jamaica a place fit for the home of the white man. Without it, the place would be a fever-ridden land of pestilence, p. 49.

Now it is into this region of the globe so hostile to the most vigorous European life—that Anglo-Saxon incuriousness has introduced the marriage laws of Europe, with the result that during the last three hundred years very few Europeans—if any—born in those islands have achieved anything like an international reputation. And why ? Miss Burry has given the reason, viz :—

" The natives of those latitudes were born tired, grew up tired, and have been tired ever since."

Their mothers have not observed the regulation period of rest and reserve which African mothers enjoy. They were " tired " when the children were born, and the children have suffered the same inability. There have been exceptional cases of noted men born in the West Indies sufficiently distinguished to be honoured by their Sovereign with the Companionship of the Bath and with Knighthood, but these were men of mixed blood who were born practically under polygamic conditions, whose mothers enjoyed the necessary period of repose.

So even in the sub-tropical region of the United States. Before the Civil War, when the white man had full control of the black woman—and their wives enjoyed, in consequence, a period of rest and reserve—some of the greatest statesmen of the United States were born ; but since the Civil War and the black woman has become mistress of herself, the absence has been marked of any striking intellectual power.

It is on record that distinguished men of the early days of the American Republic were not ashamed to offer the hospitality of their black girls to visitors. Thomas Moore, the poet, refers to this phase of American Social Life as it existed in the higher circles in the early days of the Republic as follows :—

> The patriot fresh from Freedom's counsels come,
> Now pleased retires to lash his slaves at home ;
> Or woo, perhaps, some black Aspasia's charms,
> And dream of freedom in his bondmaid's arms.
> *Moore's Works*, London, 1853, *p. 295.*

We may remark in passing that we have had in Sierra Leone, and other West African Colonies, what we consider a great thing—and *it is something* to think of--we have had capable natives, men who have distinguished themselves, whether in theology, medicine, or law, who have been able to hold their own with the average European of similar culture, but these men—nearly all the result of the polygamic system, must be regarded as exceptions—sporadic examples—they have left in the past—and they will probably in the future —leave no successors. This is a serious fact which should be inquired into.

Another advantage of the African Marriage System is—and it is a great advantage—that in no part of Africa is there the melancholy state of things which we are told Mr. Hall Caine has set himself to combat in England.

The *Daily Telegraph* published the following :—

The problem with which Mr. Hall Caine specially deals is that which concerns woman in her human (I might almost say her sexual) relation to man, and this leads him directly to the problem of the fallen woman, " the woman of the under-world," as he calls her, " the first wife of the well-to-do," the " creature of the abyss," the " slave of the soul-market." He asks who this woman is, where she comes from, and how she is created ; and he answers ; " From the house of the poor workman, the home of the poor tradesman, the poor doctor, the poor clergyman, from the great shops of chartered libertines, where labour is cheapened by the profits of week-end prostitution, and poverty, poverty, poverty is at the root of the whole terrible tragedy."

When the author comes to the practical question of what to do with " the tramps of the West-end " he reaches the central moral purpose of his play. He says in effect, " We build shelters and doss-houses for all other kinds of outcasts, but we do nothing for the smartly-dressed, bejewelled woman who is the worst of all the victims of our social system. No respectable hotel will take her in, no decent home will shelter her ; once she has made the false step only the houses of sin are open to her."

Under the African marriage system such a state of things is utterly impossible. There are no " women of the under world," no " slaves of the abyss." Every woman is above ground protected and sheltered.

Again : we are told by English periodicals that

there are a little over five millions of unmarried women in Great Britain and the number is increasing. It is stated also that in the City of London alone there are 80,000 professional outcasts.

We are quite sure that there are not so many unmarried women in the whole of Africa between the Atlantic and the Red Sea and from the Cape to the Mediterranean.

Now, if polygamy has done nothing else it has saved and is saving Africa from all these evils. Is this nothing to be thankful for? We are not confronted by those frightful evils, which in Europe and America are the despair of the guardians of public order and the reformers of public morals.

CHAPTER V.

THE Caribs—the aboriginal race of Jamaica—in their depressing climate perished under the hard conditions to which they were subjected by their Spanish invaders. They were substituted by Negroes from Africa who also perished by thousands in comparatively short periods and their places had to be supplied from time to time from Africa. By the introduction of new blood from time to time, both from Europe and Africa, the West Indies prospered and continued to do so as long as recruits could be carried over from the old countries of men with the aboriginal racial vigour. But after the abolition of the Slave Trade and natives had to be depended upon for labour and initiative prosperity began to decline. Now the descriptions we have of some of the Islands read like accounts of a former civilisation. " Decaying harbours once crowded with shipping ; ruined wharves, once busy with commerce ; roofless warehouses ; stately buildings fallen into ruins and overgrown with tropical creepers ; deserted mines and advancing forests "— these are some of the changes.

Sir Alfred Jones is trying to rehabilitate the West Indies, but he sees that this can be done only by introducing fresh blood from the mother country —men who are not " born tired " ; and he invites young Englishmen of small capital to go out and settle there. He may succeed in effecting this inoculation, but it will only be a question of time, when, if the same marriage law continues, the offspring of the new recruits will also be " born tired," and it will again require the multifarious and invincible energy of another Liverpool Briareus for the resuscitation and regeneration of those islands.

As we said last week, Europe is not satisfied with her solution of the marriage question. We hear of vigorous efforts sometimes put forth to suppress the social evils growing out of their institutions—to rescue both man and woman from degradation. But these efforts must always be sporadic and ephemeral in their results. We quoted last week from the *Daily Telegraph* the description which Mr. Hall Caine gives of his method of curing the evil. He proposes to adapt the horrors of the social system for presentation on the English stage, but his method is glaringly inadequate and insufficient.

Dr. Rentoul, of Liverpool, in his remarkable book on " Race Suicide " recognises the increasing frailty of children born under existing circumstances. The Doctor, in his despair, prescribes as a remedy the heroic method of sterilization of the unfit products, but this is rightly objected to as not only cruel, but inadequate—as a one-sided and temporary remedy—only cutting down the tree without destroying the roots.

One remembers the tremendous efforts made by Dr. Parkhurst of New York, some years ago, to cleanse the Augean stables of that city, but he had not the power of Hercules. He soon discovered that his sentimental and enthusiastic fiction was but a vexatious and barren intrusion. The river of radical legislation was needed to thoroughly effect the object. The original freedom of man must be restored. Mercy and truth must meet together and righteousness and peace must kiss each other. The tree must be made good before the fruit can be good. If we are to trust another distinguished Divine of that city, we must believe that notwithstanding Dr. Parkhurst's indomitable and passionate philanthropy, "New York has become the wickedest city in the world." The ablest statesmen in Europe are grappling with this question, and in considering it they have in view not so much any religious obligation or any supernatural regulation on the subject as the effect which any radical change in the Marriage Laws of the country would have upon the whole fabric of their civilisation. Africa has no such fabric to maintain and happy is she that she has not, for she does not need it.

The African system is both preventive of the evils we have described and productive of the good we see on all hands among the unsophisticated natives, in the integrity and continuity of their social life. It is when the decaying life of the natives in the Colonies is set beside the living and

vigorous figures that come from the interior that
the system intruded upon us from Europe appears
out of place and wickedly incongruous. Still there
are many in Europe even in these days of scientific
progress, when new light is being every day thrown
upon the "Foundations of Belief" who think that
Africa must be made to conform to the European
idea of religion and society before she can be saved,
in spite of all the proofs to the contrary which a
hundred years of expenditure of life and treasure
have furnished. Canute may command the retro-
gression of the waves, but the rebellious surf
continues to advance in spite of the Imperial
inhibition.

There are, however, other Europeans, who live
in Africa, and engage in practical work either
as political administrators or commercial exploiters, who recognize the disadvantages which
accrue both for their work and the good of
the native himself, from the attempt usually
made to evangelize him. They see that to
Christianize the native after the ordinary European
fashion, is to ride roughshod over the ruins of
splendid physique and a noble energy—to make
the native helpless and useless—in spite of
numerous brilliant exceptions—for the great work
to be done in and for his country.

There are not a few who pretend to ignore these
facts. But they belong to the ostrich school of
thinkers, who imagine they annihilate facts by
refusing to look at them. But we are glad to
know that there are many who see—and their
number is increasing—who have ceased to be
ostriches because facts are too strong for them.
They have been closely watching their teachers,
with the result that they decline to look upon their

authority as unimpeachable. They no longer look
upon them as they did in the past, with something
of the feeling with which the people of Lystra
regarded Paul and Barnabas. (Acts 14). The
great things the converts were promised have not
been realized by their awakening life. The cord
of love which it was supposed and which they were
taught would bind them together as a result of
their religious training has proved a rope of sand.
Everything and everybody is drifting.

Chapter VI.

Industrialism.

Having endeavoured to describe the basic unit of
African society, viz. :—the Family, and to show how
this is organised, and the effect of this organisation
upon the animal life—the vitality and perpetuity of
population, we now proceed to point out, as far as
can be done in the columns of a newspaper, how
the African has provided for the employment of
the energies and the support of this population
from the day of birth to the day of death ; so that
under the African system there is no widespread
pauperism, no " submerged tenth," no waste
products.

Just as the African has learned his eugenics
from the animal kingdom—the necessity of reserve
and recuperation in the female, so in his indus-
trialism he has learned the principle of co-operation
from the insects. "Go to the ant thou sluggard,"
said the wise man, "consider her ways and be
wise." The African has had before him that
wonderful insect called the termite and has

watched its method and its structures. Everywhere in Africa the termitarium or "bug-a-bug hill" is an object lesson to the native, and has been for millenniums. Among them these hills are regarded as sacred. The residence which the termites build for their habitation is said to have given the idea of the Pyramids to the Egyptian architects. Similar passages traverse the internal regions of the termitaria to those seen by visitors to the interior of the great Pyramid of Cheops ; leading to an open space, exactly like the Central Hall of the Egyptian monument, where the Queen bug-a-bug resides, from which she is never removed except by violence. It is said that when she has finished growing, she lays thousands and thousands of eggs every day, which the workers carry off to the nurseries ; and the little grubs which hatch out of them are looked after by the workers who act as nurses and see that the little ones are fed.

The circular dwellings of the native are also derived from the termitaria. It is said that circular dwellings are found in Central and South America, only among the natives of Guiana where termitaria of large size abound. Mr. H. W. Bates, late Secretary of the Royal Geographical Society, says that he never saw one termitarium on the Amazon.

It is from this object lesson we gather that the industrial system of the African is derived. It is co-operative not egotistic or individualistic. *We*, and not *I*, is the law of African life. Indeed the word civilisation, invented by the Romans, has its root in this idea. They adopted the maxim of Marcus Aurelius who said, "That which is not for the interest of the whole swarm is not for the interest of the single bee." The word civilisation derived from

two Latin words *cum* and *eo*, means coming together
or going together. This is the idea that underlies
the efforts of the better class of Socialists in
Europe—a socialism which says—not that all yours
are mine, as a dominating and exclusive principle,
but all mine are yours ; and aspiration toward this
great end is growing, as we see from a recent
telegram from London :—

> There are to be 1,200 Socialist candidates at the Municipal
> Elections in England, as compared with 722 last year.

Mr. Robert Blatchford, in his book entitled
" Not Guilty," says :—

> In the absorption of the " I " by the " We," that is to say by the
> tribe lies the root of all ethical thought. The self-asserting
> "individual" came much later on. . . . In the constant ever
> present identification of the unit with the whole lies the substratum
> of all ethics, the germ out of which all the subsequent conceptions
> of justice, and the still higher conceptions of morality, grew up in
> the course of evolution. . . . .
> The selfish instincts come down to us from our earlier brute
> ancestors.

The optimistic poet of England, Mr. William
Morris, foresees the time when the selfish instincts
will be entirely eliminated :—

> For that which the worker winneth
>   Shall then be his indeed,
> Nor shall half be reaped for nothing,
>   By him that sowed no seed.

> Then all mine and all thine shall be ours
>   And no more shall any man crave
> For the riches that served for nothing
>   But to fetter a friend for a slave.

Under the existing social order of England, the
Prime Minister has declared :—

> That twelve millions of men, women and children are in England
> living on the verge of starvation.

And Mr. Chamberlain stated that :—

The ordinary conditions of life among a large proportion of the population are such that common decency is absolutely impossible.

By their socialistic and co-operative method in all material things, the African system avoids all this. The main business of a tribe—all the families co-operating—is to provide sufficient food, clothing, house-room, and all the conditions of a reasonably comfortable life for all—even the slaves—who are really domestic servants, children of the household, such as Abraham and other patriarchs possessed—are provided for.

The conditions which have secured these comforts to the African from generation to generation throughout the centuries are—first, the collective ownership by the tribe of all the land and water ; second, the equal accessibility of these natural objects to all—man, woman, and child.

The people have free access at all times to the land and to the water, to cultivate the land for food and clothing, to hunt and to fish. All land animals, birds, and insects useful or harmful to man, are theirs to enjoy or to destroy without let or hindrance.

Everybody has the right to sail upon river, lake, or sea and retain for his own use and benefit every thing which may be the result of his efforts in these elements. There is no law of property so sacred that any man, woman, or child would be allowed to remain and suffer either hunger or nakedness without a sufficient supply of food or clothing provided such things existed in village or community. When villages or towns become too crowded the whole population turn out and build other towns in the vacant places around. We have ourselves been witness to such improvements in the countries in the interior, where we have seen places cleared and buildings erected by the co-operative method for the accommodation of three to four hundred persons in one week.

When the full meaning to the life of the African of the two conditions we have mentioned above, as regards land and water, is understood, then it will be realised why the African everywhere fights for his land when he will hesitate to fight about anything else.

It is in view of these facts that so much apprehension is felt for the future of Liberia as a State in Africa composed of African Colonists. The settlers born and brought up under the individualistic ideas of the West could not understand and hardly yet understand that there is an African Social and Economic System most carefully and elaborately organised, venerable, impregnable, indispensable. Indeed, until very recent times, even the British Government, which has always been most sympathetic in its dealings with Africa, did not recognize that there was an African social organisation, which influences every phase of African life, from the cradle to the grave, as we said above ; and Miss Kingsley has done more than any other single individual to bring this important fact to the knowledge of the British people.

Thinking Europeans see the failure of the egotistic and competitive system which it has been attempted to introduce into Africa, and readily admit its utter incompatibility and viciousness.

Miss Kingsley, in calling attention to the

importance of the land question among Africans
says :—

I have no hesitation in saying that the finest of all African
natives, the true Negroes, whose home-land is in West Africa from
Gambia to Cameroon, can be made as loyal and as devoted to
England as the man in the street up here, provided you do not
make two mistakes in dealing with them to-day. One mistake is
giving him, unintentionally I am sure on your part, an agrarian
grievance ; any gentleman, even a white gentleman, one of the
truest white gentlemen ever made, and one of the bravest—the Irish—
when he has an agrarian grievance in his mind is not a comfort to
the Empire or himself. It will be the same with the true Negro if
you give him now for the first time, mind you, an agrarian
grievance. Buying and selling him from people from whom he
thought you had the right to buy him never shook his love for
England ; but go and take away his own land in his own home-
country when you said you would not, in treaties and by word of
mouth for more than a hundred years ; go and make him, without
consulting him, a tenant-at-will where he was once absolute holder,
and a trustee for his future generations in the bargain, and you will
give him an agrarian grievance ; and how he feels about it he
explained to you in the Hut Tax War in Sierra Leone.—*West
African Studies*, p. 434.

CHAPTER VII.

INDUSTRIALISM.

NOT only in Africa, but in all countries, the economic and social systems are in large measure
derived from the teachings of Nature. The climate
of Europe compels to incessant labour. The gods
— such as Odin with his hammer— force the people
to work and to fight. The native of that climate
gathers his industrial proclivities and his restless
activities from the asperities of his natural environment ; and he expects races living under more
genial and indulgent climatic conditions to exhibit
the same inextinguishable fervour that he does—to
understand and appreciate what he chooses to call

the "dignity of labour." What his gods compel him to do he reconciles himself to by giving it a beautiful name, though in his less poetic moods he uses another phrase, the "drudgery of labour." It is a fortunate temperament which enables us to invest the disagreeably inevitable in attractive euphemisms. "The Art of putting things" was interestingly discussed by a Scotch essayist some years ago. But the drug retains its qualities, however thickly enveloped in sugar.

The "dignity of labour" is glorified, however, only among those who have various means, either in their surroundings or in their prospects, of alleviating or brightening it. The idea is not of common acceptation. To the millionaire there is "dignity in labour"; to the hod-carrier there is only drudgery. The *Spectator* (October 5), strongly reactionary on this subject, is obliged to admit that "the subordination and discipline of labour, in pursuit of the material objects of civilisation, have their *painful* aspects." All that glitters is not gold.

Civilisation as it exists in practice is quite contrary —really antagonistic—to the original and radical idea of the word as we pointed out last week. Its modern tendency is to beget classes and masses— to emphasize the *I*, and suppress the *We*, to create the capitalist and the proletariat ; and is a constant struggle between the "top and the bottom dog." Renan, the great French critic and philosopher, declared that "civilisation has always been a creation of aristocracy, upheld by a small number."

The same disasters which the competitive or egoistic system produces in England and throughout Christendom it produces in Africa even on the small scale on which it has hitherto been able to operate—happily only in the coast settlements.

These deplorable results flow from the individualistic order as naturally and regularly as showers from the clouds of summer.

If, therefore, Europe wishes to help Africa—and in her own interests she must wish to help Africa— she can do so effectively, as Sir Alfred Jones has recently suggested, only by assisting her in the maintenance and development of her own social system.

There was a time when the native African, brought up on European lines, looked upon everything European as absolutely superior, and as alone indispensable to the attainment of man's highest happiness and usefulness in this world, and even to salvation beyond the grave. He looked upon the European method of accumulating wealth, the wear and tear and excitement of trade, upon the banking system, the individualistic possession, as the *ultima Thule* of human development. But a vast, a sad, an increasing experience has proved to him, so far as happiness for himself or success for his posterity is concerned, that these things are but "broken cisterns that can hold no water."

Not one civilised native, who fifty years ago was, for this country, independently rich in the European sense, has left any descendant who is not to-day living from hand to mouth ; and there is no prospect that things will be any better in the future. The African is, therefore, rapidly arriving at a revision of his former immature ideas on the subject. There are to-day hundreds of so-called civilised Africans who are coming back to themselves. They have grasped the principles underlying the European social and economic order and reject them as not equal to their own as means of making adequate provision for the normal needs of all members of society both present and future—from birth all through life to death. They have discovered all the waste places, all the nakedness of the European system both by reading and by travel. The great wealth can no longer dazzle them, and conceal from their view the vast masses of the population living under what they supposed to be the ideal system, who are of no earthly use either to themselves or to others, and the great number of human beings from whom these "waste products" are recruited generation after generation. And these so-called civilised Africans are resolved, as far as they can, to save Africa from such a fate. They observe that in the social structure of Europe there are three permanent elements — Poverty, Criminality, Insanity—people who live in workhouses, prisons, and lunatic asylums. These are at the bottom of society, and from these issues what the *Spectator* (September 24, 1904), describes as :—

The miasmatic fluid which oozes out from below the foundations of all the great civilisations.

Above these and rising towards the surface of Society, are the "submerged tenth," who live partly by work and partly by crime, Above the submerged tenth, we find the great mass of working men who can only provide for their necessities from day to day during the working years of their lives, and whom the workhouse stares constantly in the face as a final resource. *(See Appendix C.)*

Now under the African system of communal property and co-operative effort, every member of a community has a home and a sufficiency of food and clothing and other necessaries of life and for life ; and his children after him have the same advantages. In this system there is no workhouse and no necessity for such an arrangement. Although according to European ideals the people live on a lower level, still there is neither waste nor want, but always enough and to spare. They have always the power and the will for a generous hospitality. Lieutenant Cameron, who wrote "Across Africa," told the present writer that when on his celebrated journey from the East Coast with a number of followers his supplies gave out before he had completed half the journey and he had no means to purchase food, the natives —men whom he had never seen before and whom he never expected to see again—furnished him, free of charge, with all the provisions he needed until he reached the Atlantic. Mr. H. M. Stanley tells a similar story.

These are the people whom imaginative Europeans denounce as "lazy" ; but all over the continent, where they are not disturbed by the moral depredations of unappreciative foreigners, they realise and have in daily practice the reform which Mrs. Bosanquet tells us is much needed in England. "What we want," she says, "is a reform which will provide suitable food and care for the children—from the first day of their lives, and continue to provide it throughout manhood and old age."—*Contemporary Review*, January 1st, **1904.**

CHAPTER VIII.

INDUSTRIALISM.

THE communistic order of African life is not the result of accident. It is born of centuries of experience and is the outcome of a philosophical and faultless logic. Its idea among all the tribes is enshrined in striking proverbs. Among the Veys, for example, a proverb runs thus, " What belongs to *me* is destroyable by water or fire ; what belongs to *us* is destroyable neither by water nor by fire." Again : " What is *mine* goes ; what is *ours* abides." And this proverb never fails in illustration all over Africa. Among Mohammedans the Koran comes to the help of this principle by its remarkable utterance in the Chapter entitled the Spider. " Surely the frailest of all houses is the house of the spider," referring to the egotistic method of construction and purpose. Miss Kingsley recites an African legend, illustrating the saying of the Native that " The White man is a great spider."

In England at the present moment, there is a fierce struggle to get back to the African idea and practice in social economy. One of the most serious effects of the individualistic land system in England was forcibly described in the debate on the Scotland land question in the House of Commons, April 30, 1907, by the Lord Advocate, who said that " the land used exclusively for sport was approximately three million acres. He was reminded of Tennyson's lines—" And so there grew great tracts of wilderness, Wherein the beast was ever more and more, And man was less and less." Mr. Gilbert Slater has just published a remarkable work entitled, " The English Peasantry and the Enclosure of Common Fields," in which he says :—

The suggestions borne into my mind for the agricultural policy of the twentieth century may be summed up in the phrase, *British Agriculture must be democratised.* By this I mean that the principle of collective ownership of the soil must be established or re-established ; that agricultural co-operation must be revived in new forms suitable to modern conditions ; that the ancient right of independent access to the soil for every tiller of it must be restored, etc.

Mr. Sidney Webb, in a Lecture on the 17th of last month on the subject of " Where Socialism Stands To-day," said :—

Socialism was to his mind not a panacea ; it was simply a theory of the economic organization of society. It afforded a clue to difficulties and a guide to their solution. Socialism was the outcome of all the economic thinking of the century, and the whole course of events tended towards it. He never troubled as to which Minister dealt with Social or Economic problems, because, whoever the Minister was, he was bound to arrive at a solution on more or less collectivist lines. The whole experience of Government during the last seventy years showed that no intelligent person could look on the existing state of society without indignation.

Mr. H. G. Wells in the *Grand Magazine* for September, insists that private ownership is only a phase in human development, necessary and serviceable in its time, but not final. He says :—

The idea of the private ownership of things and the rights of owners is enormously and mischievously exaggerated in the contemporary world. The conception of private property has been extended to land, to material, to the values and resources accumulated by past generations, to a vast variety of things that are properly the inheritance of the whole race. As a result of this, there is an enormous obstruction and waste of human energy and an entire loss of opportunity and freedom for the mass of mankind ; progress is retarded, there is a vast amount of avoidable wretchedness, cruelty and injustice. The Socialist holds that the community as a whole should be inalienably the owner and administrator of the land, of all raw materials, of all values and resources accumulated from the past, and that all private property must be of a terminable nature, reverting to the community and subject to the general welfare.

The Editor of the *Magazine of Commerce*, says, that Mr. Grayson's return at Colne Valley has brought the question of Socialism to the very fore-front, at one bound, and that it is foolish to ignore Socialism or dismiss it as a mere fad.

The property laws of Africa in intention and in practice make for the widest distribution of wealth or well being and work steadily against concentrating the wealth of a community, either of land or production in the hands of a comparatively small number of individuals.

From the Family Organisation and the property laws which naturally follow, the whole Social System is regularly developed. We have the village or the town, then the province or district— all of these together form the State or Tribe ; and the continuity of the life of these institutions follows the general principle underlying the Family Organization. There is unity, equality, and at the same time priority or paramountcy, all the groups together composing the social system. Self-government is exercised always with the Family group ; and there is also within every group recognized and acted upon this general principle, that the efforts of each and the efforts of all are and must be made for the good of each and the good of all.

Each family is responsible for the care of its own weak ones, the aged, the incurable, the helpless, and the sick. If the family fails, then responsibility falls upon the village or town, etc.

In matters of more general interest the village or town is responsible, and as the interests widen the larger and higher social groups become involved in their responsibility.

Under this system no hospitals are needed, which are necessitated by the individualistic system of Europe and America and the complications arising from foreign intervention.

Under the African system also no stealing takes place. The necessity and the habit of theft do not arise, because everybody has his rights, and everybody has enough. In travelling through London, every now and then one sees notices in railway carriages, and other much frequented places, to the following effect, " Beware of pickpockets," " 75,000 thieves in London known to the police," etc., etc. These notices are astounding comments on the social conditions, though intended only to emphasize the advertisements of Chubbs' locks, iron safes, and other contrivances for guarding the property of one man against the encroachments of another.

We cannot help feeling that one of the causes of theft is the very strenuous and ingenious methods devised to prevent it. In the interior of Africa there are no safes, and there are no thefts. Voluntary testimony by foreigners is abundant everywhere on the subject of African honesty. To mention only one or two. M. Guinand, a French Captain of Engineers, who was engaged in the construction of the Dahomey Railway, speaking of the honesty of the natives in a report, published in the *Bulletin du Comite de l'Afrique Française*, of January, 1904, says :—

I shall cite two facts in my personal experience on this point. I have lived eleven months in the midst of these people, often leaving my trunk and other effects for a whole day without any other protection than that of my boy, and never have I lost anything at all, although my house was on a thoroughfare along which a great many people pass. The other fact, even more demonstrative, is the following :—One day a labourer needing some money asked me to lend him twenty sous, which I at once gave him. When the time for payment came, this little detail escaped my memory, and I paid him the full amount of his wages. Imagine my surprise when a a few hours afterwards I saw my man hastening back a distance, which I afterwards learned of ten kilometres, bringing back the piece of twenty sous, saying that when he received the money he forgot for the moment his debt. Shall I add that I was so struck by his honesty that I gave him the money ?

Lieutenant-General Sir William Butler, G.C.B., in his book on South Africa, entitled "From Naboth's Vineyard," says :—

In all the sad history of South Africa few things are sadder than the Zulu question. Where the Zulu came no lock or key were necessary. No man who knew the Zulu—not even the white colonist—whose rage was largely the result of his being unable to get servile labour from him—could say that he had not found the Zulu honest, truthful, faithful ; that the white wife and child had not been entirely safe from insult or harm at the hands of this black man, or that money and property were not immeasurably more secure in Zulu charge than in that of Europeans or Asiatics (p. 263.)

One of the Ministers at Natal wrote to General Butler as follows :—

I think the Zulus are behaving very well in the present trouble. . . . . . It seems to me a thousand pities that such a splendid race as the Zulus ever came into contact with civilisation at all. (p. 99.)

We hear of thefts and burglaries committed by aborigines in the Settlements. In their own country these people are guiltless of such crimes ; they learn to indulge in them when brought into contact with the egotistic system, which everywhere furnishes both temptation and incentive to steal, and from which Europe is now endeavouring to escape.

Nothing in Native life of value is ever really destroyed by European indiscriminate interference, but everything is made weaker. Some things unrepressed by philanthropy or legisfaction continue to operate, albeit clandestinely, in their worst forms. The African marriage custom, for example, never abandoned, continues in its most degrading animal aspect, and a false life is assumed, poisoning the social atmosphere and undermining the moral character. The substructions of the social and moral structure being impaired, the whole building is shaky, and no man can depend on his neighbour. So much for unscientific, if good meaning, intermeddling in other people's affairs.

Corruptio optimi pessima.

CHAPTER IX.

THE PRODUCTION OF WEALTH.

THE production of wealth in Europe is communistic in the highest degree ; but the distribution is individualistic in its most intense form, hence the social unrest and discontent. The proletariat are ever on strikes—men and women not only clamouring for higher wages but for a more equitable division of the results of the communistic labour ; that is, the results which capital and labour together have produced. All combination for Industrial ꞌ purposes is co-operative, but the difficulty in Europe—we should perhaps say the impossibility—is to get an equitable share of the proceeds for each party who contributes to the result. And this is the problem which is now confronting the leaders of English society in Church and State. Mr. Asquith, in his speech on October 19 on Socialism, said :—

Any one who looked around with unprejudiced eyes at the structure of Society as it actually is, and realised not only the enormous disparities in the distribution of material comfort and happiness, but the still more striking discrepancies between opportunity on the one side, and talent and character on the other, would not only find it difficult to reconcile what he saw with even the rudest standard of ideal justice, but would be tempted to be amazed at the patience and inertness with which the mass of mankind acquiesced in what they deemed to be their lot. No wonder that constant contemplation and reflection upon such a spectacle had driven and continued to drive some of the best and finest spirits of our race into moral and intellectual revolt.

Mr. Bernard Shaw in a speech at Chelsea Town Hall referring to the subject said :—

The most important thing for the middle classes was so to use political power that no man should get any wealth unless he had taken his share in producing it, and that his share should bear some relation to the effort he had made. The man who took a share he had not produced was inflicting on the community the same injury as a burglar or a pickpocket.

The Bishop of Birmingham, in a sermon at the Birmingham Cathedral on Sunday, 22nd September, called attention to the prophetic denunciation of those who added land to land and house to house till there was no room for the poor to live, and said :—

The Old Testament was also full of condemnation of those who took the service of men and did not pay them a living wage . . . . . The real wealth of a nation did not exist in the production and distribution of commodities, but in the number of individuals who had enough to flourish on. A nation's poverty lay in the number of those whose lives were starved and stunted . . . . . There was a great moral claim for a juster distribution of the profits of industry becoming more clamant throughout Europe. The Christian Church as a whole had very little to say about it. And yet in a large measure it spoke the language of the Prophets. Why had we forgotten it ? Why had we allowed it to come from outside the Church ? There was time to make amends. We should try really to learn again the mind of our God, spoken by the Prophets, and put ourselves by the side of Christ, listen to his words, and see whether their meaning did not smite our souls.

This is also our complaint against the Church, as it has been brought to us from Europe. It has demoralised the Social System of Africa ; it has

robbed us of our communistic spirit by denomina-
tional strifes and rivalries, and is helpless to supply
a remedy; "it has put book into our head," as an
old and prominent female member of the Church
said to us last week, "and has taken love from our
heart," and yet the people, owing to their spiritual
aspirations and necessities cling to this Organisation with a loyalty and devotion which, to adopt
the language of Mr. Asquith, used in another
connection, "amazes the outsider at the patience
and inertness with which the mass of people
acquiesce in what they deem to be their lot." The
Church not only does not help, but imposes burdens
upon the people for which there is no warrant in
the system of religion as taught by Christ.

Africans living under native laws and Institutions
would never co-operate with any man or company
to the end that one man or company should
appropriate to his or their own use and benefit
the whole of the surplus wealth resulting from
their joint efforts. The whole of the surplus
wealth accumulated under our Native System
by co-operative labour is regularly and in a
most orderly manner sub-divided among all the
people co-operating, "Unto each according to his
several ability." Those whose efforts are worth
more receive proportionately a greater share of the
surplus. The internal wars of the African have
been largely in defence of his Social Institutions,
resisting men of his own tribe anxious to aggrandize
themselves at the expense of the people. His
wars against Europeans have also been in defence
of his Institutions which he regards as sacred.

Our natives who have accumulated money
under the individualistic system of Europe cannot
go back to their tribal home because their wealth

would be subjected to distribution according to native custom and law ; and in view of their training it is impossible for them to submit now to such an arrangement ; therefore they continue to live under the European Order and are amenable to its vicissitudes. All their wealth, sooner or later, goes back to the European, in spite of the most stringent provisions of Wills and Codicils. Men may doubt this, object to it, hate it, and think that their case will be an exception to the rule, but the law goes on all the same. It is not a *rule* but a *law*—the law of disintegration under the European competitive order.

Earnest missionaries in their innocence and goodwill strove from the very first to destroy the communistic order of African life because they saw that the whole system was based upon and grew out of the family arrangement, which, in their lack of scientific knowledge, and entire misconception of Scripture, they " abhorred." A distinguished Prelate once told the writer that the abolition of the African Family organization had done more harm to the permanent interests of the people than all the reputed cannibalism on the whole continent. An able and interesting writer in the *Westminster Review*, (October 1851) made the following suggestive statement, applicable with still greater force to this very day :—

It was our happy fate to spend a year at M‘Carthy's Island, about one hundred and eighty miles up the Gambia. It is not a particularly pleasant or healthy place ; the thermometer is often 106 in the shade during the dry season ; the whole island is a perfect marsh during the wet. In the year 1848 seven Europeans remained on the Island during the rainy season; at the end of it one out of seven was alive.

. . . .

The Wesleyan Missionary Society, with that amiable absurdity which characterises philanthropic exertions in Africa, attempted to form a Foolah settlement at M'Carthy's Island ; a large sum of money was expended in building a village, where no doubt warming pans and every other necessary of existence would have been provided. The whole affair was of course a complete failure. Philanthropists must learn that if really anxious to benefit a people, the good must be done in accordance with their feelings, and prejudices, and habits. And that, although the not instantly adopting a taste for tea, crumpets, and excellent exhortations, is a proof of utter barbarism ; yet it is impossible to innoculate a people with a taste for all these necessaries and comforts of civilised life at once.

This principle has long been recognized by Africans of culture. It was to this that Rev. now Bishop Johnson of Southern Nigeria referred when, in his celebrated letter to Sir John Pope Hennessy in 1872, he said : " God does not intend to have the races confounded, but that the Negro in Africa should be raised upon the basis of his own idiosyncracies."

Sir Samuel Lewis, in his Introduction to Dr. Blyden's book on " Christianity, Islam, &c.," said :—

Foreign influence may—indeed it must—for some time to come do much for Africa, but not least by recognizing the fundamental fact that, when all is said and done by Europeans and Americans that they can do, the African himself is, and must always remain, the fittest instrument for the development of his country.

We have had among us educated natives who have accumulated money on the European system and have tried to apply it to the development of agriculture on the individualistic plan. Some have spent thousands of pounds and devoted years of labour to this enterprise, have built large substantial houses with the idea of making permanent centres for their work, but all, without exception, have failed. Their habitations are now tenanted by bats and other noxious vermin. " The frailest of houses is the house of the spider."

So with Organisations among civilised Africans, whether for Industrial, Educational, or Religious work. They do not succeed. They have often been tried here and elsewhere on the Coast. They do not succeed because they violate the law of African life and growth. For, after all, they involve what might be called a plural egotism. They do not imply the *We* of the communal life. They are competitive Organisations not only to promote their own but to circumscribe the prosperity of others. Like the Combines in Europe they threaten the life of others ; and this Africa will not allow. What is *mine* goes ; what is *ours* abides.

CHAPTER X.

INDUSTRIALISM.

WE referred in our last to the serious problems by which British and other European statesmen and reformers are confronted, growing out of their social system. Statesmen, legislators, and divines are appalled by the magnitude of the task before them, and are inclined to look upon every proposal for reform even when suggested by the most expert social physicians as more or less Utopian.

The Bishop of London during his recent visit to Canada in a speech at Ottawa referring to the social difficulties in England and to the necessity for the emigration of the surplus population said :—

I know you do not want " our wasters," but you do want some of our healthy young fellows. We want you to help them to come out here and live a real man's life instead of the dog's life they live at home.—*The Guardian*, Sept. 25.

On the subject of the Houseless Poor in a letter

to the *Daily Telegraph* General Booth makes the
following drastic recommendations :—

> There are some 2,000 or 3,000 houseless poor in the City of
> London. We ought to begin then to discuss the question and the
> remedy. There they are—a torture to themselves, a disgrace to
> our civilisation, a menace to public health, the source of disease,
> filth and abominations—and they are a dreadful expense to the
> community. I say they ought to be taken away, without regard to
> their depravity or non-depravity, or whether their state is the result
> of misfortune or misconduct. Society would not allow a sheep
> bleating about the embankment dying gradually of starvation,
> covered with filth and vermin. How much better is a man than a
> sheep. Someone asked that question once, it was never answered,
> and perhaps never can be answered, and yet, here we have these
> poor wretches crawling about in this condition. *Take them away.*
> Never mind what it costs, Do it.

This is the generous and humane remedy which
General Booth offers—that great religious leader
whom thousands if not millions follow.

There is no country in Africa to which such a
description would be applicable : and there is no
African statesman who would make such a recom-
mendation. The African believes that the earth is
the Lord's and the fulness thereof, and the sheep
and the goats and the cows are all communal
property, and no sheep would be allowed to go
about bleating with filth and disease without being
cared for.

As we have said before, no African living under
African laws or African institutions would help to
forward any enterprise which would result in the
appropriation by a few of the surplus wealth
resulting from the joint efforts of the people.
When this system is introduced by foreigners the
African is antagonistic, and often prefers to go on
strike into the primeval forest, and there, under
however hard conditions, live a life of freedom

from dependence on anyone for the everyday needs of even mere animal existence. Africa fights continually against a proletariat class. Under her system there must be no exploiters and no proletariat. This is why the Native sometimes appears to the unimaginative European as lazy.

Under his native institutions the African lives for the most part out of doors, and is not overburdened with clothes. He likes light and heat. He always builds his towns near water—creeks and rivers—that he may have free use of that element for purposes of ablution. He bathes in the morning before he goes to his work and in the evening when he returns, so that there is no chance of there being produced that class of wretches whom General Booth denounces as " a menace to public health, the source of disease, filth, and abominations "; and whom he would get rid of at any cost, whatever their innocence or guilt.

When does the African study ? it may be asked. He studies every day—morning, noon, and night— from the cradle to the grave. He is ever reading the book of Nature ; and there is never chapter or page in this book which he is either ashamed or afraid to look at. He is constantly speaking to the earth, and the earth is constantly teaching him, as Job says.

It is charged against the African that he is lazy, and needs a lot of wives to work for him ; and yet a hundred steamers constantly dog the coast to take away his produce—created not by the help or supervision of the white man. He is lazy, yet steamers frequently lie in West African ports for days landing cargo. All this stuff must be presents to a lazy and worthless set of men, who give nothing in return. How benevolent our kind

friends in Europe must be! But let us examine
the charge, looking into the daily life of the people.
The man has to fell all the timber on the land, and
prepare the ground for building or farming. He
has to build the house for the wife. If he has six
wives, he has to build a house for each of them.
The women sow the seed, and the men and women
reap the crop. In cloth manufacture the women
spin the cotton, and the men weave. Everywhere
there is this division of labour. All work. But
the men everywhere always do the hardest and
most exhaustive forms of labour. For recreation,
the women have no Hyde Park to go to and drive
their carriages ; but after the daily work, the
evening bath, and the evening meal, they decorate
themselves, and indulge in various native dances.
Free from undue anxiety, they literally " take no
thought for the morrow," knowing that the earth
will constantly yield her increase sufficient to
supply all their needs.

The African has no expensive Army or Navy or
great Civil Service to maintain, so he does not
need to perform unremitting work to keep up
these destructive and unproductive institutions.
With him work is not the object of life, but life is
the object of work. He does not live to work, but
he works to live. Labour with him, as with all
other men, is a curse. Occupation is a blessing.

Now, from what we have been saying during the
last few weeks, it will be apparent that we do not
wish to see the communistic and co-operative
system of Africa disturbed by indiscriminate
foreign invasion. And here we would ask those
who have done us the honour to follow us thus far
in this discussion, whether in social, economic, or
industrial life, Europe has anything better to offer

to the African than the system he has constructed
for himself?

CHAPTER XI.

THE CRIMINAL IN AFRICA.

A RECENT number of *The Times* (December 10,
1907), informed us that an important statute
affecting the administration of Criminal Law
passed at the last Session of Parliament would
come into operation at the beginning of this year.
In nearly all the foreign periodicals that come
daily to hand there is some reference to crime and
the difficulties of dealing with it.

Africa has no such problem. As a rule, only
the crime of murder or high treason is punished
with death; for these are regarded as offences
committed not against any individual but against
God and the State. Other crimes such as theft,
etc., are punished by deportation, the criminal
being allowed after a term of years to return to
his country. Criminals, who, after due examina-
tion, not according to individual caprice, but
according to established traditional law well
known to the people, are not always executed
immediately, but are reserved for some
appointed time when all persons proved
worthy of death are gathered together in some
public place, where, with the sanction of religious
rites, they are executed before God, as
Samuel hewed Agag in pieces before the Lord, and
as David delivered to the Gibeonites the seven sons
of Saul to be hanged before the Lord in expiation
of their father's crime ; and this was done under the

authority of Jehovah, the Supreme Ruler to whom alone vengeance belongs.

Now the Africans in punishing criminals attach a sacred significance to the act. They do not regard it as their own doing, but the Lord's. The criminals and all the people are brought into the presence of the Almighty, who they feel takes cognizance of all the actions of men, and who as Judge of all the earth will by no means clear the guilty.

We often see in foreign papers great horror expressed at some public executions in Africa, which are ignorantly described as arbitrary human sacrifices and attributed to the blood-thirsty disposition of native Rulers, as if men anywhere would delight in the shedding of blood as a mere pastime.

The Africans by their penal method produce a deterrent effect upon the people, at the same time that they rid the country of the pernicious influence of the permanent criminal class, which the system in England, for example, of long or short imprisonments for certain crimes does not do. It neither deters the people from crime nor saves the community from the example, as well as the taint of criminality. In the article in *The Times* referred to above, it is said :—

In thinking of the professional burglars who are at large by reason of misplaced mercy or indulgence, the outlook seems dark. . . . . . Courts seem to be guided by radically different principles. In the same community may be two Judges, sitting at no great distance from one another and acting in systematic antagonism ; the one seeming to think that punishment is generally an expensive mistake, the other convinced that it ought to be given in no frugal spirit. Men who go from one Court to prison are in another let out on their recognizances. Some Judges and magistrates are not a little responsible for the perplexity of the public as to the proper treatment of criminals. It is quite possible that there may be equally great diversity of judicial practice in applying the new Act. To prevent this, there could be no better way than to have informal conferences among the authorities responsible for its working as to various matters, including the important question as to the stamp and class of persons who are to be appointed probation officers and the exact nature of their duties. We want something different from a mixture of a policeman and a relieving officer. A great experiment is about to be made, and it is essential that it should be carried out with intelligence, tact, and uniformity.

The practice in Africa is to rid the country both of the crime and the criminal. Now the result of the European system is that some of the worst criminals are incarcerated for a few months and then let out to continue to poison the moral and social atmosphere. The method does not seem to be to extinguish the burglar, but to invent instruments to defeat his enterprise. Every day in England the magistrates are sending hundreds of culprits to prison, and every day hundreds are released, a large proportion of whom before that week or even before that day is ended will have again commenced a course of conflict with the law and may not impossibly be again undergoing punishment. In a word, the result of the European system of indulgence, discipline, and retribution, is that Europe passes through the gaols a vast number of criminals who become as active and as dangerous an element on their release as before their capture. These men were criminals before they went to gaol and they resume the life of crime the moment they are let out, on whom, moreover, the punishment which they have just endured has had no reformatory effect, for no moral influence was brought to bear upon them during their period of incarceration.

Mr. H. B. Montgomery, in a recent number of

the *Nineteenth Century and After*, an ex-prisoner himself, tells us of a prisoner who had been in gaol for about twenty years, and who during that time had not had one moment's spiritual or moral instruction. Every day, then, hundreds of foes to the interest and peace of the community are turned loose, only to return to a career of war upon society. This is perfectly well known to the Police, to the Gaolers, and to the Judges. " Be careful," said a magistrate to us in this city before whom we were prosecuting a criminal who had robbed us and by whom we were being cross-questioned. " Be careful how you answer that man's questions, for he is an old hand at it." The Magistrate had seen the prisoner before several times. It will be seen, then, that unfortunately for us, we have among us some features of English criminal practice. The " 75,000 thieves known to the Police in London," are of course ex-prisoners who have undergone discipline or retribution in the prisons.

The African system, on the other hand, while it deprives the criminal of the power of doing further mischief, safeguards the community by its effective deterrent influence.

The fact is that the African periodical "Customs" as they are called, and ascribed to inveterate barbarism and cruelty peculiar to Africa, were at one time practiced in Europe by all the nations who now lead in civilisation. The practice of human sacrifice prevailed in all parts of Europe even among highly-cultured people. Men were sacrificed by the most prominent and by even the most educated individuals. At a military sedition Julius Cæsar ordered two of his soldiers to be publicly killed as expiatory offerings by the High Priest and the Priest of Mars and fixed their heads before the

Regia Martis. The Gauls sacrificed men at every important crisis at the time of Cæsar and Cicero. The old Swedes every nine years, at the great National Festival, celebrated for nine days, offered nine male animals of every chief species, together with one man daily. The Danes assembling every nine years in their capital sacrificed to their gods ninety-nine horses, ninety-nine dogs, ninety-nine ducks, ninety-nine hawks, and ninety-nine men.

Among Africans these periodical customs, no longer practiced, were of the nature of sin-offerings on behalf of the whole community and thank-offering also for the national deliverance from the fact and taint of crime. We fear that no such thoughtful or pious motive enters into European executions, where the criminals are either slaughtered privately or made the sport and jest of the populace.

CHAPTER XII.

THE CRIMINAL IN AFRICA.

OF all the charges brought against the African, perhaps the most serious is that of blood-thirstiness as was supposedly exemplified in the Annual Customs which formerly took place at Ashanti, Dahomey, and Benin. The execution of large numbers of prisoners on various occasions has been generally represented as being the wanton indulgence of a natural or racial instinct in cruelty perpetrated upon innocent and harmless victims.

But the world has within the last few years—in

this enlightened twentieth century—been shocked
by the sanguinary proceedings in highly civilized
Europe. The papers have described wholesale
executions which have taken place there. The
number of persons said to have been hanged at
Warsaw in Russia alone at one time was six
hundred. We have also all read of the unprovoked
massacres at Kishnieff and other places of un-
offending Jews. Are we to suppose that these
people were killed as a religious duty with no
feeling of bitterness or revenge ? Yet the method
of the African in their penal arrangements has
often been made an excuse by their foreign
exploiters for slaughtering them wholesale, killing
more natives in one day in innocent blood than the
African system kills in criminals during many
years. This is the way an unenlightened civilisation interferes to save the natives.

Now if any executions or massacres approaching
such as have occurred in Russia had taken place in
Africa the news would have been heralded abroad
as an example of inveterate and unmitigated
savagery.

Owing to an entire misconception on the part of
foreigners, a great deal has been made of what has
been called the " Annual Customs," which have
existed, and perhaps still exist among some of the
African tribes, when the extreme penalty of the
law is to be carried out.

Among some of the tribes, criminals who have
forfeited their lives are reserved for a special day
in the year when the Rulers of the People meet to
make sacrifice for the sins of the Nation by
disposing of the criminals who have been sentenced
to death, under the sanction, and with the approval

of the highest religious authorities. Crime is never said to be punished by the fiat of the King, but by the Judgment of God, to whom alone the people believe that vengeance belongs, and who only has the right to recompense. Compare this deliberate, calm, judicial, religious taking of life with the stories of lynching which come from the Western World or of Pogroms which come from Russia; and remember that one is the practice of benighted heathen in the European sense, and the other of enlightened Christians. If the modern superficial critic of African Customs would only read history, he would find that that great nation who gave law to the civilized world—Rome—in its most brilliant period, after Virgil, Cicero and Horace had lived, and the reign of universal peace had prevailed under Augustus,—practised most brutal customs; he would discover that hundreds of highly civilised people gazed periodically from the benches of the Coliseum upon the combats of men with men, between whom no enmity existed, or of men with beasts. Roman spectators encouraged men to butcher each other, not under the influence of any cause so respectable as superstition, but from a morbid love of amusement at the sight of blood. There were women among the spectators who sat and applauded, and with wild outcries urging the populace to refuse the petition of the kneeling gladiator, giving the signs of murder to the guards of the arena. If the censurer of African customs read further and came down to the time when Christianity had taken possession of Southern Europe, he would observe that among the sportive recreations of highly-cultivated Spanish Christians, was the shedding of blood, sometimes on behalf of Christianity; they would see a bull-fight in the list of amusements at Seville or an *auto-da-fe* in the square at

Toledo. They would gaze at an amphitheatre thronged with spectators ; the King is on the throne ; Torquemada sits beside him on the dais, and the banners of the Inquisition float beside those of Aragon and Castile. The Cathedral has sent its Chapter and its Choir ; the monastery, its sable or white-robed brethren ; the grandees are surrounded by their suite ; the beauty and the chivalry of the realm are sitting side by side ; and in the outer circle is an indiscriminate crowd, eager, jubilant, and uncontrollable ; the vacancy in the midst is occupied by upright stakes, on which are bound a Mohammedan, a Jew, and one who, though neither Jew nor Mohammedan, has been reading feloniously a book written fifteen hundred years before by certain fishermen of Galilee.

Now we want to ask whether Africa has ever exhibited to the world any such scenes as those described above. The religious training of the perpetrators of these deeds cannot be said to have been neglected. Their deeds cannot be ascribed to their secular in contradistinction to their religious training.

CHAPTER XIII.

RELIGION.

WHAT is Religion ? Generally the answer is that which makes a man feel that he is not his own guide, judge, or ultimate authority ; that he is bound to a higher and irresistible Power that created him and by whose *fiat* he will cease to live. That is religion. He may have no conception of the nature or character of the Power ; and leave him to himself without external influence or the aid of books, he will never even try to define to himself what that Power is ; he only knows it exists—I AM—and is sufficiently impressed by the reality of its existence, whether looking within at the workings of his own mind or without at the operations of Nature. He knows that a power not himself is working within and around him, and not to offend this power and to gain its favour, he uses various means which appeal to his untutored imagination to effect this object. All races without the Bible and even with the Bible have their own method of approaching this Being.

The African believes that the great Being can be approached through every object which he has created, whether animate or inanimate. He can conceive of nothing which is not instinct with the Creator. He is a Pantheist, which Miss Kingsley used to say is a form of her own Religion. He never attempts to formulate any conception of the great Creator and hence he has no theology ; but that he is a spiritual being all close observers of his condition admit.

Mr. R. E. Dennett in his work entitled "*At the Back of the Black Man's Mind*" says in his Preface :—

I wish to show that, concurrent with fetishism or jujuism, there is in Africa a religion giving us a much higher conception of God than is generally acknowledged by writers on African modes of thought.

. . . .

The lasting effect of missionary effort in Africa must depend to a very great extent on the grasp the missionaries are capable of attaining of this higher conception of God which the natives of Africa, in my opinion, undoubtedly have, and the use they may make of it in manifesting God to them as the one and only true God and not merely as the white man's God.

Thirty years ago Professor Max Muller pointed

out as theory what Mr. Dennett endeavours now after careful study on the spot to demonstrate as a fact. It is not difficult to believe that the researches of Mary Kingsley and those of her disciples owe their inspiration largely to the philosophical and scientific disquisitions of the Hibbert Lectures :—

I maintain, says Professor Max Muller, that fetishism was a corruption of religion, in Africa as elsewhere, that the Negro is capable of higher religious ideas than the worship of Stocks and Stones, and that many tribes who believe in fetishes cherish at the some time very pure, very exalted, very true sentiments of the Deity. Only we must have eyes to see, eyes that can see what is perfect without dwelling too much on what is imperfect. The more I study heathen religions, the more I feel convinced, that, if we want to form a true judgment of their purpose, we must measure them, as we measure the Alps, by the highest point which they have reached. Religion is everywhere an aspiration rather than a fulfilment ; and I claim no more for the Religion of the Negro than for our own, when I say that it should be judged not by what it appears to be, but by what it is—nay, not only by what it is but by what it can be and by what it has been in its most gifted votaries.—*The Hibbert Lectures* p. 195 (1878).

It is certain that Religion originated in Africa. It went from Ethiopia, that is to say, from Negroland eastward and northward to Egypt and down the Nile, extending to the heart of Asia. All representations of Buddha which we have seen are painted black.

Lady Lugard, in her work on "A Tropical Dependency," says, p. 17 :--

When the history of Negroland comes to be written in detail, it may be found that the kingdoms lying towards the Eastern End of the Soudan were the home of races who inspired rather than received the traditions of civilisation associated for us with the name of ancient Egypt. For they cover on either side of the Upper Nile, between the latitudes of 10 deg. and 7 deg. territories on which are found monuments more ancient than the oldest Egyptian monuments. If this should prove to be the case, and the civilised world be forced to recognise in a Black people the parent of its original enlightenment, it may happen that we shall have to revise entirely our view of the Black races, and regard those who now exist as the decadent representatives of an almost forgotten era, rather than as the embryonic possibility of an era yet to come.

From our standpoint, we do not believe that Africa needed the theological interference of Europe, for the Theology of Europe is derived from the conceptions of Roman, Celt and Teuton, which have modified the Semitic ideas promulgated in the Bible. European Christianity is Western Christianity—that is to say, Christianity as taught at Nazareth, in Jerusalem, and on the Mount of Beatitudes, modified to suit the European mind or idiosyncracies What Africa does need from Europe is its Imperial and scientific help, ruling from the "top of things," as Miss Kingsley said ; and directing in the material devolopment of the country. But for spiritual leadership in Africa, the events of a hundred years of effort do not justify her interference. This was what Lord Salisbury meant when he said " Missionaries are not popular at the Foreign Office."

We published in our last issue a most interesting letter from Bishop Johnson of Western Equatorial Africa, which we were very glad to get. The Bishop is nothing if not outspoken—always fearlessly uttering his convictions. Although brought up in the creeds of Europe yet his African instincts and experience teach him to say :—

3. We have for a long time now been contending, and that rightly too, for a teaching and training that shall not destroy our Native African idiosyncracies and that will not Europeanise us, but I fear we are practically giving over our contention now.

We Africans in our pure and simple native state know not any distinction between what is secular and what is religious. With us, there is nothing secular. Religion enters into every department of life with us, and so it should be with beings who know that they are responsible to the great Author of their existence and of all creation also for everything they do, and that they are expected to seek His glory in and through everything they do.

Our Native African education and training have always been based upon that form of Religion professed by the country originally and which is reckoned among all those forms that we Christians speak of as heathenism. An attempt on the part of professing Christians and other Religionists to secularise school education for our youths and dissociate from it the teaching of religion is plainly and entirely un-African.

Yes ; it was by taking advantage of the religious spirit of the African that the alien missionary first established his hold upon the people. Our only difference from Bishop Johnson is this—that throughout his entire able letter he seems to identify Religion with European Theology. Religion, as we said at the outset, is that which binds us to a higher Power, and is practised by men of all climes and countries. Theology is our conception of and our attempt to describe the Being worshipped, Who has no name. What He is to one race, He is not in every respect to another. " I am that I am," or " I shall be that I shall be," is His own definition of Himself. Religion is the ocean, theology the river. All rivers flow into the ocean, but the ocean is not the river, and the river is not the ocean. The African does not attempt to formulate a Theology. He says, as the Psalmist did, " Such knowledge is too wonderful for me ; I cannot attain unto it." This is the Semitic and Hamitic attitude of mind.

Now, as to the practical results of the European system, so far as we have received it ; Bishop Johnson deplores the lack of ability and character of the youth trained under the Missionary system. He tells us :—

As I travel about in the course of my business in the country— Yoruba, the Niger Delta, Denin, and other parts of Southern Nigeria which have been the scene of my labours now many years,

I find that with Government officials and European merchants, native Christian young men, including Sierra Leoneans, as assistant workers are much at a discount now. Not much confidence is placed in them for downright honesty and integrity. There is scarcely any European mercantile factory in the River Niger district where native Christians as book-keepers or officers filling other very important posts are to be met with as had once been the case. These posts are commonly filled now by Europeans.

I leave a broad margin for that unreasonable prejudice which many a European on the Coast has often entertained and manifested against the Negro simply on the ground of his colour, as if it is a sin in any man that he wears the colour of skin which the Creator has given him, as if there is any excellence in the white colour *per se,* and for the need that has induced many a white man to seek employment in West Africa and whose urgency may sometimes lead an unprincipled person to seek to prejudice a neighbour's interest to get himself in. Still, I find that many of our young people have often given cause for the unfavourable opinion referred to above, and here and there I have met with overworked Native merchants who would like to have some very reliable important assistants to share with them the higher responsibilities of their business establishments to afford them the relief which they feel the need of, and which may tend to prolong their lives, but who have often found it extremely difficult to find such persons.

On the other hand, Mr. Percival Mayall, Director of Education for the Colony of the Gold Coast, in his Report made in August last, says that :—

" Almost the whole of the scholars come to school with their fixed aim and object in life to become a clerk or to hold a similar position." The Report voices the prevalent opinion that the present system of education tends both to encourage a distaste for manual labour in favour of clerkships and to create an exodus from the country districts into the Coast towns.

Now here we have the testimony of a high dignitary of the Church and of a Government Official lamenting the disappointing, if not disastrous results of the education given to the people, chiefly by missionaries. All these young men at school must have been taught the Bible, or must have received religious instruction ; yet the Bishop s surprised and grieved at what he considers the prospective danger of the secularisation of the schools. What is to be done? Were these boys taught the Bible or the creeds, Religion or Theology?

CHAPTER XIV.

RELIGION.

WE closed last week with a quotation from Bishop Johnson as to the general effect so far of foreign training upon the youths of West Africa. It is difficult to get our philanthropic friends to understand that as a rule, the training they have been giving to the Negro with the very best intention is not the best for him; that, in many respects, it disqualifies rather than fits him for comprehending his proper relation to the outside world and his own peculiar work. They honestly give us their best and wonder that their best does not produce the best results; but their best on their line is not as good as our best on our own line. There is but one way open to every man and every race for effective life and successful work; every other channel is full of difficulties and obstructions. That only way must be found out before there can be peace and harmony and progress. Among the best Imperial Administrators now of West African Colonies there is a serious and earnest effort being made to study and codify native laws on all the various subjects that affect native life. This is the method that must be pursued before any efficient education can be imparted to the natives.

The missionary work as pursued at the present day is not the same as that pursued fifty or a hundred years ago. We have now " the steamship and the railway and the thoughts that shake mankind." We have a multiplication of news-papers and books that reach the native who has learned to read the English language. In former days the missionary had what may be called a *tabula vasa*—an open and uncontested field. What he told the people remained in their mind as absolute truth, based, not only on the Word of God, but coming from a country where the people had reached the perfection almost of angels, and therefore he had a right as one of those who had "already attained" to be the guide of others. But all this is changed now. Natives frequently visit Europe and see things for themselves; and for those who remain at home the effect of what the foreign preacher says on Sunday as to religion and morality is neutralised on Monday by unsavoury reports brought by the news-papers from the country whence the teacher came. The native becomes incredulous and begins to think about the mote and the beam. Besides this, the pressure upon the time of the native; the fierce competition with foreigners on his line of work—his means of livelihood; the exigencies of the steamship and the railway, often necessitating work on Sunday; the example of lay Europeans taking their pleasures on the sacred day; all these things leave the native no time and less disposition to listen to what the missionary is trying to tell him. It is evident, therefore, that without a thorough revision of missionary methods, adapting them to changed conditions, missionary work in West Africa will become more and more impossible.

Then, again, those who study the question notice that there is increasing and rapid degeneration among the natives who come in contact with the efforts that tend to Europeanise them. *They are dying out.* Their children are frail, weak, insipid, physically, mentally, and morally. Recent reports from Uganda, where missionary work was supposed to have produced such wonderful results, are sad reading. *The Record* newspaper for December 6, 1907, reports an interview with Archdeacon Walker, who has laboured there for twenty years, in which the Archdeacon made the following distressing statement :—

It may be startling to describe the Buganda, the hope of Africa, as a dying nation ; it is perfectly true. In 1901 the total population of the kingdom of Uganda was estimated at a little over a million, to-day it may be put at 700,000. If the death-rate be not stopped the whole population will die out in twenty years.

These melancholy statistics it is evident were not in the possession of Mr. Winston Churchill, when he made his remarks the other day on progress in Uganda.

Similar decay has followed the introduction of philanthropic work in Hawaii, Fiji, Madagascar. The French are now employing vigorous measures to suppress alien interference with the religion and customs of the natives in Madagascar, and thus save their lives and preserve their mental and moral integrity.

Religion with the African in his pure state concerns all classes of the people, and as we said in our last, he approaches God by all the various means which He has created. They believe that the divine powers inhabit stones, trees, springs, and animals ; and we find traces of this kind of worship in the Bible and in the early history of the Greeks. We find, for example, a sacred stone at Bethel called the House of God. There is a sacred oracular tree at a place called Sichem (Gen. xii. 6). Then there are the sacred wells at

Kedesh and at Beersheba to which people went to find God. In earliest times amongst the Greeks the image of a god was nothing but a mere stone which served to represent the deity and to which offerings were brought. This was the primary origin of altars. The example of stone worship may be seen any day in the Timne country. It is true, as Heber says, that—

> The heathen in his blindness
> Bows down to wood and stone.

But he does not look to the stone for help. He recognises within and beyond that stone the Spirit of his Creator.

CHAPTER XV.

RELIGION.

OWING to the intense and increasing materialism of Europe, especially Anglo-Saxondom, the people have lost touch with the spirit world. This is no reason why Africans should forget the privileges enjoyed by their fathers. The inter-communion between the people of the earth and those in the spiritual sphere is a cardinal belief of the African and will never be uprooted. Death is simply a door through which men enter the life to come or the Hereafter. This being the basis of their faith they have, like the Japanese, no dread of death. Some years ago in our hinterland the people thought no more of despatching one of their nearest relatives to the spirit world than we now think of sending a messenger to a friend in one of the neighbouring villages. At Mano-Salija before the advent of civilisation the bar of the river was considered one of the chief entrances to the abode of the spirits. This impression still remains amongst the people, only their spiritual leaders think that this gateway has been polluted by the advent of strangers and strange customs. It is said that about fifty years ago when the Vey country was under great affliction by war from the Interior tribes, and man-stealing by the Spaniards was at its height, the people, decided to send one of their number—of royal blood—of the lineage of the King and Prophetess —into the world of spirits—to relate the story of their affliction to their ancestors who in their turn would represent it to the Supreme Being. This was also a custom among the Japanese. It is even said that they deposited beside the corpse letters of credit to be honoured in the next world.

We have learnt from a Vey Chief, that there are to-day in the Vey Country sacred places of worship near springs and creeks and rivers. A place called Zontomy is said to be the most wonderful for exhibitions of specimens of the reptile kingdom which may there be witnessed. No one finds the Zontomy unless accompanied by the living prophetess. On the day of the Banquet of the Dead when thousands of people go to make offerings to their ancestors (consisting of rice, flour, cassada, grain, meat, not fish) these things are placed before the prophetess on the sandy shores of Zontomy Creek. The visitor, who is a stranger, is alarmed when at the call of the prophetess, a frail little woman, a huge crocodile comes to the surface of the water and in a straight line makes towards the crowd. On reaching the shore she is fed with flour in the presence of all. It is really astonishing to see a tiny old woman passing her fingers through the dreadful teeth of this monster. After this, other crocodiles come one by one as they are called by name by the prophetess. In a few minutes the whole surface of the creek is ruffled by the upward shooting of the heads of fishes and crocodiles. The food is then indiscriminately distributed over the surface of the water. The Marfah Bay, Qualu creek at Bendu, and Sugary are other sacred places. At Sugary the Sandfish family meet their sacred dead and a huge crocodile still guards the place, and the people move freely among them. At any of these places one may at any time see the prophetess going down under the surface of the water remaining there over an hour, then coming up attired in the most gorgeous fashion, her hair plaited, beads tied all over her limbs in a most artistic manner.

At these places intercourse with the world of spirits is constantly carried on. Everywhere in Pagan Africa there is this intercourse. In Europe many people are trying by various methods to get back into intercourse with the spiritual world. Many at the present day believe that

Spiritualism has given more proof of a future existence than any other ism, showing clearly that the so-called dead can and do return, and that their presence has been manifested in every home, as apparitions, ghosts, in omens, warnings, dreams, various strange sounds, and in various other ways. There are members in every household in England who have had visitations of the so-called dead, but they have put it down to fancy or imagination ; they could not conceive in their own minds that spirits could return to earth again, especially as they generally appear in the clothes they wore before passing away, this being of course essential for recognition. These are facts that cannot be disputed.

The Rev. R. J. Harrison, D.D., Vicar of St. Thomas's, Newcastle, preached on the subject of " Spiritualism," taking his text from St. Luke

16-31.   He asked his hearers as to how spiritualism stood :—

"God," he said, "was a spirit, and if we worshipped Him we worshipped Him as a Spirit." In the next place there was a spiritual universe in which the spirits were as real as the stars in heaven. In this spiritual universe there appeared to be constant movement. Men's eyes, in the Bible, were said to be opened and to have beheld the movement of great spiritual armies. . . . . Spiritual phenomena of real value were as broad as humanity and of everyday occurrence ; but we have lost the power of recognising the phenomena. There were a few men and women here and there who were able to know the phenomena when they occurred, and understood their nature ; that was the reason why mediums were of so much importance. We had lost the faculty because we have lost the inclination. The majority of us were not half good enough to be spiritualists. We were not spiritually-minded ; we thought more of eating and drinking than of fasting and prayer. More of the glory and pomp of this world than of discovering the glory and dignity of the other world. . . . The reality of the phenomena is becoming more and more certain, and the region of investigation has become enormously large.

Spiritualism is penetrating into the higher circles of Society. We find in *The Tribune* for January 10th the following, contributed by a correspondent at St. Petersburg under date January 9th.

The Tsaritsa has been again seized with a serious nervous indisposition as a result of protracted spiritualist seances and the shock caused by the recent accident to the Imperial yacht, the Standart. The doctors insist upon the Empress taking a long and absolute rest in Italy.

Mr. Casely Hayford, in his valuable book on "Gold Coast Native Institutions," tells us of a visitation of spirits in the graveyards on the Gold Coast. He says, pp. 103-105 :—

I shall not soon forget a scene I witnessed in a grave-yard on the Gold Coast not long ago. A widow had just lost her son, whom I knew. He had belonged to a friendly society, and at his burial the "brethren" had brought flowers for the bier. A few days afterwards I noticed this woman come to the grave of her son, who had belonged to the Church, with the usual food and drink for the dead. But she had brought something else—a bunch of flowers.

Surely her son would want the flowers—would like them. I saw her— a simple native woman, who, probably, in all her life, had never loitered by the wayside to wonder at God's simple daisy—amidst her tears, gently place the flowers upon her son's grave.

On another occasion I was lingering in the same grave-yard by the side of a figure of "Hope," my thoughts far away from the immediate surroundings. Suddenly a women's voice addressed me : " *Ye wura ahaö : awuraba su ahaö*," meaning " Master, good day ; and you too, mistress, good day ;" I was startled, at the strangeness of the salutation ; and, before I could recover my senses, she had slowly walked away. So fervent is their belief in the hereafter. To them man never dies.

Now, when the missionary comes along, simple soul that he is, and gives the would-be converted native the comprehensive command to give up all fetish as a thing abominable in the sight of God, his reason reels, and the foundations of his faith are, for the first time, shaken. But he soon finds himself on *terra firma*, and when he remembers the lessons of his youth and considers that, after all, the missionary may be wrong in a matter that affects the vital interests of the life beyond, he remains for ever afterwards only a Christian worshipper in form, if he does not openly revolt. Where he remains a formal worshipper, it does not necessarily follow that he is a hypocrite. The fact is that he likes the music and the ceremonials of the Christian Church, and would fain continue to enjoy them, while at heart he remains true to the faith of his fathers.

So you may change the Theology of a people, but you cannot change their Religion. This is especially true of the Jew and the African.

The African Religion is a matter that affects all classes of the people—men, women, and children. As a Pagan, the women assist in the functions of Religion, which are the functions of the State. They visit the sacred groves. The Bundo and Porroh rites act conjointly with the State in training the youths of both sexes to morality and patriotism. As in other matters, the Religion is communistic. When this system is recklessly and indiscriminately interfered with, the result is what we are witnessing everywhere in West Africa, as in Uganda—dislocations, degeneracy, death.

APPENDICES.

APPENDIX A.

BARRISTER HAYFORD ON THE RACE QUESTION.

To the Editor of the *Weekly News.*

DEAR SIR,—I have followed, with keen interest, the series of articles on "African Life and Customs" in the Sierra Leone *Weekly News* from the ever-instructive pen of Dr. Blyden ; and, perhaps, the following thoughts, suggested by them, may be useful to the student of African problems, seeking for the conditions suitable for Race Emancipation.

I believe it was the learned Doctor who first pointed out that Africa needs no spiritual interference from without ; but that she requires emancipation from the thraldom of foreign ideas, inimical to racial development, few will doubt. What, indeed, can be more certain than that the African in the United States, in the West Indies, and in the mother country, east, west, and south, has need to unlearn a good deal ? But the unfortunate part of it is that the way out is as yet but dimly dawning even upon such as would otherwise be qualified to lead the masses. It becomes, therefore, the sacred duty of those who can see a little more clearly ahead to point the way. Hence it is that, in season and out of season, the warning voice of our grand old man is heard.

The African, who comes to his brethren with red-hot civilisation straight from Regent Circus, or the Boulevards of Paris, and cries anathema to all black folk who will not adopt his views or mode of life, is, perhaps, not the man who is, or can be, of

much help in developing African life and African
idiosyncracies along the line of natural and healthy
development. That is, perhaps, the underlying
teaching, if not the sum total of the teaching, of
the series of articles now before us.

Africa seems destined for ever to be a land of
mystery. When, in our modern way, we have
demolished African strongholds, and with the
wantonness of an iconoclast, saved nothing to
remind us of the artistic past and future possibilities of the people—nay, when we have laid out
streets and encouraged shops to spring up mush-
room-like here and there, we think we have solved
the mystery of the gods, while, all the time, the
heart of the matter is not reached. In many a
forest glen they dwell in their tens and in their
hundreds, but seldom in their thousands, undis-
turbed by the vulgar eye. Your cities are not their
cities, your tinsel is not their gold. All they ask
for is for as little interference as possible. What
can you do with such a people, except to give them
scope and room for natural development ?

I am writing this on the verandah of a house in
the main street of the modern town of Kumasi.
Where once stood the palace of the King, now
stands an ugly coast building with dirty blinds and
a dirtier shop below. But the men and the women
are not changed. The type is pronounced ; and as
I watch them passing up and down in different
groups, it is easy to see that the men and women
who walked the banks of the Nile in days of yore,
are not far different from the remnants of the sons
of *Efua Kobi*. As you see the new unfinished
coast houses side by side of the frail, impermanent,
quadrangular compounds of the old type, the
thought suggests itself to you that, after all, it

is the intangible that matters. You enter
one of these compounds, and you find but bare
open rooms, in the case of a chief's house often
supported by pillars. Where do these people
actually live? Where do they keep their treasures
and their household gods? No one can tell you.
But they are as safe as the Golden Stool itself is.
Thus you arrive at the heart of these people, and
you are inwardly persuaded that all the symbols of
European authority, responsibility, and opportunity
are more impermanent than the frail houses you see
about you. How to reach the heart of such a
people would not be an uninteresting study. If
you succeed, you have arrived at the heart of the
principle which may be safely applied to healthy
race development wheresoever necessary.

Once more, then, Ashanti is my type, for the
reason that Ashanti is yet unspoilt by the bad
methods of the missionary.

I remember once seeing Rev. Ramseyer in
Kumasi. He told me he had laboured in Ashanti
off and on for forty years. I asked how many
Ashantis he had in his church at Kumasi proper?
He said thirty. His assistant corrected him, and
said fifty. I asked him how many in all Ashanti?
About two hundred. Not quite so many, his
assistant concurring. Rev. Asare, the assistant,
and his good wife are both Africans, who have
adopted the European habit. I had visited the
missionaries in my African costume. They agreed,
including my African friends, that it was appropriate. I hope the object-lesson was not without
significance to the hopes of the success of their
mission. But however that may be, to-day the
Ashanti goes as unconcerned of the white man's
religion and of the white man's ways as ancient
Egypt might have done.

What is religion ? If it is that which links back
the finite to the infinite, the material to the
spiritual, the temporal to the eternal—that which
inspires an unfaltering faith in a life beyond the
grave, then, I maintain that the African, in his
system of philosophy, gives places to none.

Hark ! what are those suggestive words I catch
from the so-called Fetish chant that the priest,
called to attend a dying man, is humming in a low,
doleful voice :—

> *Midan Yami, Kwiaduampon,*
> *Midan yami, Kwiadu,*
> *Yami ama, yami ama,*
> *Yami na wama mi akom.*

Meaning :—

> On God I depend, the impregnable rock,
> On God I depend, the impregnable rock,
> God has given, God has given,
> God has given me the priesthood.

I have loosely rendered the word "Kwiadu-
ampon" as "the impregnable rock," but, etymolo-
gically, it conveys the idea of "the ever faithful
God."

Now, when, in the face of all this you tell the so-
called pagan that he will not end well, that he is
the devil's own, he listens curiously, and wonders
whether you can mean all you say. His attitude
henceforth is a defensive one, seldom antagonistic.
Henceforth he only asks to be let alone. And yet
people wonder that so-called spiritual work makes
such little headway in these parts. And the land
had rest forty years. Do you not see the purport
of it all ? It has not pleased the gods to disturb
her. Leave her in peace, the slumbering sphinx,
until the God of Ethiopia wakes her up. For it is

not so much religion that she wants as knowledge
—knowledge that will enable her to explain to the
waiting world the faith that is in her and the
reason of her being.

According to Dr. Freeman, in his History of
Europe, the word pagan originally meant a countryman, and, by extension, a worshipper of false gods.
Well, Paul, before the application of the phrase,
spoke of a temple with the inscription to the
unknown God, whom men ignorantly worshipped.
Evident, therefore, it is that a pagan is not
necessarily a worshipper of false gods.   Even
Marcus Aurelius persecuted the Christians ; yet it
is conceivable that had he lived in a later age he
would have set his philosophical sayings in terms of
Christianity.

If Christ and God are one, those who worship
God ignorantly, worship Christ ignorantly, and it
were better for the many to worship in spirit and
in truth that which they know not fully, but as it
were through a glass darkly, rather than don the
intellectual garb which ends in questioning the
Divinity of Christ, and by parity of reasoning,
according to the theologians, the Divinity of God.

In the philosophy of the West African there is
no reason why Christ should not be God ; for to
him man is half God and half man.   But a thin
veil divides the finite from the infinite, and when
Death pulls aside the curtain, there is no knowing
what one shall be.   Indeed, it is conceivable that
paganism, scientifically and intelligently inter-
preted, may place the Christ on a higher pedestal
than Christianity has yet done.   What the unspoilt
educated African feels he wants is, rest—rest to
think out his own thoughts, and to work out his
own salvation.

Have we, who advocate these views, lost faith
in Christianity ? It does not follow.   It was
Dr. Blyden who wrote in the "Significance of
Liberia," these remarkable words :— . . . "I
am sure that Christianity, as conceived and
modified in Europe and America, with its oppres-
sive hierarchy, its caste prejudices and limitations,
its pecuniary burdens and exactions, its injurious
intermeddling in the harmless and useful customs
of alien peoples, is not the Christianity of Christ.
But I am sure, also, that the Christianity of Christ
is no cunningly devised fable—no *ignis fatuus*—to
disappear in darkness and confusion.   I am sure
that its spirit will ultimately prevail in the proceedings of men ; that the knowledge of the Lord
shall cover the earth as the waters cover the sea.
I am sure that Jesus, upon whom is the spirit of
the Lord, because He hath anointed Him to preach
the Gospel to the poor, to heal the broken-hearted,
to preach deliverance to the captive, the recovery
of sight to the blind, to set at liberty them that are
bruised ; I am sure that this

> Jesus shall reign where'er the sun
> Does his successive journeys run.

. . . .

" I am sure, also, that all counterfeits, however
bright or real they look, must vanish as the truth
appears.   We should not be discouraged because
the system bearing the name of Christ makes no
progress on this continent—that it lingers, halts,
and limps on the threshold of a great opportunity.   Jesus is lame.   He has been wounded in
the house of his friends.   We must bind up his
wounds.   Treading in the footsteps of our
immortal countryman, we must bear the Cross
after Jesus.   We must strip him of the useless,
distorting and obstructive habiliments by which he

has been invested by the materialising sons of Japhet. Let Him be lifted up as he really is that He may be seen, pure and simple, by the African, and he will draw all men unto Him."

The broader outlook upon religion is the lot of the careless Ethiopian. He need not necessarily see God except through Christ, but is, withal, so catholic that he can speak of the universal :—

> . . . strife that won our life
> With the Incarnate Son of God.

A significant marriage took place in Sierra Leone in March of the present year. A highly cultured African gentleman was married to a Mohammedan lady. Of this lady the *Weekly News* of March 21, 1908, says :—" There has been no attempt to unmake her, no inducement to make her alter the religion of her fathers or her native dress." I remember overhearing an argument in a railway carriage between two educated Africans as to the effect of such marriages. They were both Sierra Leone men ; and the sore point with one of the controversialists was as to how her ladyship would be received at Government House, or how she would receive at home the friends of her lord and master. Here you have the two warring elements in national development : " What is it that the white man expects me to do ? " " What is it that I am called upon in reason and by nature to do ? " Between these two the manhood of the race is throttled and sacrificed on the altar of convenience.

Now, what appears remarkable in Sierra Leone would not be remarkable on the Gold Coast, where it is common for educated men to mate with less privileged women. And the reason, founded on common sense, is not far to seek. Between the African woman who, collecting firewood on a plantation, overpowered by Nature brings her little one into the world, soothes it, and carries it safely home with her load and the African lady who talks of going *home*, meaning Europe, to be confined, there is a mighty difference. The latter is the product of an effete system of training, and it and the system will perish out of hand. The former has a foundation in character that will bear the weight of the ages as far as African life and work are concerned.

With respect to marriage a great blunder has been committed by the meddlesome missionaries, namely, "that of forcing a life of hypocrisy upon those whom they compass earth and sea to get into the fold. Whereas the average so-called convert was, before he came into the Church, living a fairly decent, open life in his marital relations, embracing Christianity invariably meant for him adopting subterfuges and chicanery to cover up the way of the old life, which not all the spiritual graces could help him to brush aside."

There is a vulgar way of approaching the question of polygamy; there is the scientific way; and lastly there is the spiritual way. It may appear strange to the average man that there is a spiritual side to polygamy. Yet on second thought it must be so. In this, as in other matters, evil be to him who evil thinks.

The crux of the educational question, as it affects the African, is that western methods denationalise him. He becomes a slave to foreign ways of life and thought. He will desire to be a slave no longer. So far is this true that the moment the

unspoilt educated African shows initiative and asserts an individuality, his foreign mentor is irritated by the phenomenon. In September 1905 public events on the Gold Coast led me to write in the local press as follows:—" We feel, secondly, that the educated native is unduly maligned for party purposes. It is the same cry as the educated Welsh, Irish, or Scotch. In any case, it is a childish cry—a sign of weakness. Does a native cease to be a native when once he is educated?
. . . . But for the educated native, where would the unsophisticated native be? Hence the weakness of the cry—the shibboleth of the ' educated native.' Heaven grant that the educated native may never be wanting in his duty to his less privileged brethren or betray their trust in him."

But let there be no mistake about the matter. The foregoing strictly applies to the unspoilt cultured African. The other type is no good to anybody. The superfine African gentleman, who at the end of every second or third year, talks of a run to Europe, lest there should be a nervous break-down, may be serious or not, but is bound in time to be refined off the face of the African continent.

And now I come to the question of questions. How may the West African be trained so as to preserve his national identity and race instincts?

As a precautionary measure, I would take care to place the educational seminary in a region far beyond the reach of the influence of the Coast. If I were founding a national University for the Gold Coast and for Ashanti, I would make a suitable suburb of Kumasi the centre. But why do I speak of a national University? For the simple reason that you cannot educate a people unless you have a suitable training ground. A Tuskegee Institute is very useful in its way : but where would you get the teachers unless you drew them from the ranks of the University trained men ? And since even the teachers must be first locally trained, the highest training ground becomes a necessity.

I would found in such a University a chair for History ; and the kind of history that I would teach would be universal history, with particular reference to the part Ethiopia has played in the affairs of the world. I would lay stress upon the fact that while Rameses II. was dedicating temples to " the God of gods, and secondly to his own glory," the God of the Hebrews had not yet appeared unto Moses in the burning bush ; that Africa was the cradle of the world's systems and philosophies, and the nursing mother of its religions. In short, that Africa has nothing to be ashamed of in its place among the nations of the earth. I would make it possible for this seat of learning to be the means of revising erroneous current ideas regarding the African ; of raising him in self-respect ; and of making him an efficient co-worker in the uplifting of man to nobler effort.

Then I should like to see professorships for the study of the Fanti, Hausa, and Yoruba languages. The idea may seem odd upon the first view ! But if you are inclined to regard it thus, I can only point to the examples of Ireland and Denmark, who have found the vehicle of a national language much the safest and most natural way of national conservancy and evolution. If the Dane and Irish find it expedient in Europe, surely the matter is worthy of consideration by the West African. Says Mr. James O. Hannay, writing on the work of the Irish League and the influence of a national language in the November, 1905, number of the *Independent Review*, at pages 311 and 312, " Our history, our customs, our character are unintelligible to us until we know it. Character, for instance, is the result of inheritance and environment ; and there is no more subtly influential environment than the language we speak. If these two are in opposition, if a people inherits a Celtic spirit and grows up in an Anglo-Saxon atmosphere, with the English language on its lips, what kind of character will result ?   It is likely that a people tossed in this cross sideway of contradictions will tend to develop inconsistencies of character— amazing force rendered useless by recurring spasms of weakness, brilliant intellectual capacity sterilised by inability to grasp the conditions of material progress ; and so forth."

If you want a further support to this view, you have it laid down in an interview with Mr. A. G. Fraser (Trinity College, Oxford), the Principal of Trinity College, Kandy, Ceylon.   Says the *Times* reporter, " He laid special stress on the importance of conducting the training given in Indian Colleges on a vernacular basis rather than through the medium of English, as is too often the case at present.   The system existing in most missionary and Government schools tends distinctly to separate those thus educated from their own race.   He advocated education almost on Japanese lines—i.e., a thorough teaching of English as a subject and literature, but the teaching of science, engineering, medicine, &c., through the medium of the vernacular, and not of English—with a complete connection between the village school and the central college."

Moreover, I would make this seat of learning

so renowned and attractive that students from the
United States, the West Indies, Sierra Leone, and
Liberia, as well as from Lagos and the Gambia,
would flock to it.   And they would come to this
Mecca—this *alma mater* of national conservancy
not in top hat and broadcloth, but in the sober
garb in which the Romans conquered the material
world, and in which we may conquer the spiritual
world.

Now, it is easy to see that the graduates that
such a school will turn out will be *men*—no effete,
mongrel, product of foreign systems.

When some three or four years back I had the
pleasure of accompanying Dr. Blyden to the Royal
Academy he drew my particular attention to a
famous picture, representing the wolf and the lamb
as dwelling together, &c.   After we had both
drunk in the beauty of portraiture for a while, he
gravely remarked, "And a little child shall lead
them—that is Africa."   I was struck by the
allusion, and I still think there is a deal in
the reflection.   But it has since struck me also,
that it is not the spoilt educated African that may
be expected to help in the regenerative work of the
world.   The unspoilt son of the tropics, nursed in
a tropical atmosphere, favourable to the growth of
of national life, he it is who may show us the way.

The voice of the ancient universal God goes
forth once more, Who will go for us, Who will
show us any good ?   May there be a full, free, and
hearty response from the sons of Ethiopia in the
four quarters of the globe !

CASELY HAYFORD.

Anona Chambers, Tarkwa,
    Gold Coast, May 5, 1908.

APPENDIX B.

The question of Eugenics is now coming prominently before the European public. Lord Rosebery in an address before the Society of Comparative Legislation (June 30, 1908) said that the science of Eugenics is greatly taking up the higher minds of the country.

The *Nineteenth Century and After* (June, 1908) says :—

"Eugenics, whatever may be the meaning of the word, is now decidedly in the air, and its study is proving more attractive to many than watching, through the medium of the daily press, the turns and twists of party politics. . . . A good deal of this infantile mortality is due to the little regard paid to the condition of the mother when she is 'carrying the child.' In France there are a number of municipal *Asiles* in which expectant mothers, whether married or unmarried, may obtain the rest which is, as every *sage-femme* knows, absolutely necessary for them."

" . . . . Now, whether the life of an individual human being is healthy or the contrary depends upon two things : (1) whether his parents were healthy ; (2) whether the environment he himself encounters is favourable to his development."

The African adds a third : whether the mother enjoyed the proper rest and reserve during the period of "carrying the child" and during lactation.

The *Socialist Review* (June, 1908) says :—

We no longer can hope to improve our race, by educational appliances from without — the improvement has to come, from within. It is the germ-plasm that matters in heredity, *and not the environment.* According to Weismann all inheritance is due to the continuity of the germ-plasm which hands down the characteristics of individual species and race from one generation to the next . . . . . If Weismann's conclusion be valid, says

Professor Pearson in his *Grammar of Science*, and all we can say at the present is that the arguments in favour of it are remarkably strong—no degenerate and feeble stock will ever be converted into healthy and sound stock by the accumulated effect of education, good laws, and sanitary surroundings.

This question was discussed with gratifying grasp and sympathy on the second day of the recent Pan-Anglican Congress, under " Marriage in Heathendom." (See *Times* Report, p. 23.)

Professor Flinders Petrie, in the *Hibbert Journal* (July, 1908), in a striking article on " The right to constrain men for their own good," writes of polygamy in an instructive and common-sense way.

APPENDIX C.

An Indian lady, who has lived for some time in England, has, in a striking work, recently published, described the hopelessness of the situation as follows :—

When I came to England, eight years ago, there was just beginning the public outcry about the unemployed. The Salvation Army and the Church Army have been at work many years. It is not far from twenty years ago that "General" Booth wrote his wonderful book "Darkest England and a Way Out," which startled the world, and which travelled, perhaps, to every English-speaking country. He hoped—in fact, I think he declared—that, given a certain sum of money, he would be able to convert "Darkest England" into a realm of light. Since the book appeared that sum of money has, I believe, been subscribed many times over, but I venture to say that if the slums he describes have some of them been wiped away others, no less hideous, have taken their places, and the dwellers in these plague spots are as unlovely, as wicked, and as hopeless as those described in "Darkest England."

There are, situated in the East End of London, countless missions sending out devoted servants into the midst of these unhappy people, and yet evil is rampant among the poor, and society grows no better ; indeed, so bad is it, that the abuse of the smart set has become a cult," etc., etc.—Miss Olive Christian Malvery, in "The Soul Market," Chap. xx.